THE STORY OF
Lafayette

"*Youth, health, fortune; the favor of his king; the enjoyment of ease and pleasure; even the choicest blessings of domestic felicity—he gave them all for toil and danger in a distant land, and an almost hopeless cause; but it was the cause of justice, and of the rights of humankind.*"

—JOHN QUINCY ADAMS

*Gilbert did not need spurs to make Victor
run like the wind*

THE STORY OF
Lafayette

By HAZEL WILSON

Illustrated by EDY LEGRAND

ENID LAMONTE MEADOWCROFT
Supervising Editor

PUBLISHERS Grosset & Dunlap NEW YORK

To

STELLA CLEMENCE

who is fond both of France and of America
this book is affectionately dedicated

Contents

CONTENTS

Illustrations

ILLUSTRATIONS

THE STORY OF
Lafayette

Soon they were in sight of the château

CHAPTER ONE

The Great Beast of the Forest

"BE CAREFUL!" said Henriette to her cousin, Gilbert. The young Marquis de Lafayette had almost tripped over his father's sword. It really was much too long and heavy for a boy of eight to carry.

Gilbert and Henriette had trudged a long way from Château Chavaniac. This was the big house in France where they lived with Gilbert's grandmother and two aunts. But, hot and tired though he was, Gilbert was not ready to go home.

"Let me carry the sword for a while," offered Henriette. "I'm a year older than you are, and I'm taller, too."

Gilbert's hazel eyes flashed. "Of course you can't carry my father's sword!" he exclaimed. "Suppose the great beast should come out of the woods! How could I kill it if you are carrying the sword?"

"I don't think anybody really expects you to kill it," said Henriette. "When we walked through the village the peasants took off their hats because you're the nobleman who owns the land they live on. But I saw them smile at each other the way grownups always do when they think we're just playing."

"I'll show them I'm not playing," declared Gilbert stoutly.

As they left the sunny fields and entered the gloomy forest, Gilbert did not feel quite so brave. He was still sure, however, that it was his duty to kill the cruel creature which had been carrying off pigs and lambs from the farms. It was a dreadful monster, the peasants said, that lived in the woods. A monster with fiery eyes and a horrible snarling roar.

A branch broke with a sharp crack. Was it the beast? Was he coming after them? Something rustled! Something fell!

"What's that?" cried Henriette.

"Shh!" ordered Gilbert.

Gilbert wanted to be like his father, who had been killed in a battle when Gilbert was two years old. Though he could not remember his father, Gilbert knew he had been very brave.

"My father would expect me to be brave, too," thought Gilbert. And he willed his feet to go forward into the dark woods.

The noises grew louder. More branches snapped.

"It's getting late. Time to be going home," said Henriette. She had had enough of this expedition.

"A brave Frenchman never runs away from danger," cried Gilbert. His face was flushed, and his red hair was nearly as bright as a candle in the gloom of the woods.

"Let's go back," begged Henriette. "They say this monstrous beast eats children."

"Come out, you cowardly beast! I'll cut your heart out. I'll rip you apart," yelled Gilbert. Then, sword in hand, he ran toward the noises they had been hearing.

[5]

The heavy sword was too much for the boy to manage. It caught in a branch. In wrenching it out, Gilbert tripped and fell.

Fortunately for him, no savage animal came crashing through the woods. Instead, when Gilbert jumped to his feet, he saw just another boy. The boy was busy breaking the dead branches into pieces small enough to be carried.

At sight of Gilbert and Henriette, the boy put his knuckle to his forehead as a sign of respect. But he did not act friendly. His clothes were dirty and ragged. He shouldered a load of wood too large for a boy of his size to be carrying.

"Why do you take such a heavy load?" Gilbert asked him.

"Because it takes a lot of branches to make a fire," said the boy sullenly, and walked away.

For a moment Gilbert wondered how it would feel to be a peasant boy instead of a young nobleman. Then he thought again of the savage beast he was hunting. "We must go deeper into the woods," he told Henriette.

"Come out, you cowardly beast!"

They had not gone far, however, when they heard somebody call, "Gilbert! Gilbert! Hallo! Gilbert!"

Gilbert recognized the voice of Abbé Fayon, who lived at the château and taught Gilbert his lessons. "He's worse than a hunting dog at tracking me," Gilbert complained.

"Oh, here you are," said Abbé Fayon, catching up with them. "You children shouldn't go so far into the woods. You might get lost."

Gilbert explained that he was going into the woods to track the great beast.

"So that's why you brought your father's sword, Gilbert," said his teacher kindly. He took the weapon from him. "You will have to be older before you can use a sword this size," he added.

"When I'm older I'll go to war," boasted Gilbert. "I'll kill plenty of the enemy with my sword."

"Suppose there isn't any war?" said Henriette. "What will you do then?"

"If there isn't a war here in France, I'll go find one somewhere else," declared Gilbert.

"In the meantime, my boy," said his teacher, "you'd better hurry home. Your mother has just arrived from Paris. She was hardly out of her coach before she asked, 'Where's Gilbert?' and I came to find you."

Gilbert did not need urging. He loved his pretty mother and looked forward to her visits. But he wished she lived with him all the time, instead of just coming to see him now and then.

Soon he and Henriette and Abbé Fayon were in sight of the round towers of the château. Gilbert ran ahead when he caught sight of his beautiful mother standing in the doorway.

"Mother!" he cried, rushing toward her.

"My little mouse, my great big boy!" she exclaimed, bending down so he could kiss her soundly on both cheeks. "You're looking well, my little cabbage. But how you've grown!"

French mothers often called their children little mice and little cabbages. But Gilbert thought he was too old for such silly names now that he was eight.

[9]

"Mother," he said, standing as tall and straight as he could, "I've just come back after almost killing the great beast of the forest."

"My brave little soldier!" said his mother, hugging him. She led him into the château.

That night, as a special treat, Gilbert and Henriette were allowed to eat dinner with the grownups. Gilbert wore his best suit of dark blue velvet with gold embroidery on the collar. His mother liked to see him dressed up. So did his aunts and his grandmother. They smiled at him when he sat down at the long table beside Abbé Fayon.

Even fifty flickering candles could not light the corners of the big dining room. A dark tapestry, which pictured men out hunting, hung on the wall directly opposite Gilbert.

The room suddenly seemed gloomy to the boy. He looked at his mother, so pretty in her blue silk dress. "I think I'll leave here and go to Paris to live with you," he told her.

"But, Gilbert, what would I do without you?" cried his grandmother.

"You wouldn't have me to play with in Paris," said Henriette.

[10]

"My brave little soldier!"

Gilbert's mother spoke to him gently but firmly. "We have talked of this before, my son. The doctor still insists that the country is better for your health than Paris would be. Be patient. It won't be long before you've grown big and strong enough to come to Paris."

"It is always the same story," Gilbert thought with a sigh. "Wait till I am big and strong." He took a large second helping of the crisp fried potatoes which a servant was offering him.

"Gilbert grows to be more and more like his father," said his fond grandmother.

Gilbert felt his mother, his aunts, his grandmother, and Henriette all looking at him. He had a feeling that they expected him to grow up to be strong and brave like all the other brave Lafayettes. Then he thought of something he had not yet told his mother.

"I have a new pet," he told her. "It's a baby lamb, and I've fed it ever since it was born. I believe it would miss me too much if I left it to go to Paris right away."

CHAPTER TWO

His New Home

C OME back to see us soon," said Gilbert's grandmother, wiping tears from her eyes with her lace handkerchief.

"Send me a letter," begged Henriette.

"I will. I will," promised Gilbert.

He was fond of his dear relatives but he was impatient to be on his way. His trunk was already strapped to the back of his mother's coach, which was waiting in the courtyard. At last she was taking him to live with her in Paris. He felt sure that he was now as big and strong as any boy of eleven in all of France.

The spirited horses pawed the paved courtyard until sparks flew. The coachman climbed to his seat, and took up the reins.

[*13*]

"Good-by! Good-by!"

Gilbert's aunts, his grandmother, Henriette, and the servants were all waving. Gilbert waved back, yet he could not feel sorry to leave them. He was happy to be on his way to Paris. "Going to Paris, going to Paris, going to Paris," the wheels of the coach seemed to sing all the way.

Gilbert's first sight of Paris amazed him. He leaned so far out of the coach, in order to see the city, that he nearly fell into the road. He had never dreamed that Paris was so big.

"I could walk a week and not see half of it," he told his mother excitedly.

At last the coach stopped at the magnificent Luxembourg Palace, where Gilbert's mother lived with her father and her grandfather.

"This must be the grandest palace in the world," cried Gilbert, as he helped his mother from the coach.

"The King's palace at Versailles is grander," said his mother. "But this is grand enough."

Gilbert looked around. He had never seen such lovely gardens. There was a large pool with golden carp swimming in it. There were beautiful fountains. Peacocks walked proudly on the velvety grass. Gilbert could hardly bear to leave the gardens and go inside the palace.

On the palace ceilings were painted pictures of ladies wearing scarves and of curly-headed angels. Gilbert tipped his head back to look at them. He tried not to stare at all the shiny mirrors and the gold chairs.

"It is much more elegant here than it is back at the château," Gilbert thought.

After he had washed, and changed his dusty clothes, Gilbert's mother took him into the big salon to meet his grandfather and his great-grandfather, and his mother's friends.

"This is my big boy, Gilbert," she said.

As Gilbert crossed the room to greet his two relatives, he bumped into a small gilt table. A statue of a dainty shepherdess fell and broke.

"He's as awkward as a young colt. It's time he learned how to behave in polite society," snapped his grandfather coldly.

Gilbert had never dreamed

that Paris was so big

At that moment Gilbert wished he were back at Chavaniac with his grandmother and aunts. He knew they loved him. But apparently his mother's father disliked him at sight.

Then his great-grandfather said heartily, "Hello, my fine fellow. Don't worry about breaking that statue. It shouldn't have been in your way. How are you, my dear boy?"

"Very well, thank you," said Gilbert, feeling that here was a friend. Gilbert gazed admiringly at the old man's splendid uniform. Although Gilbert's great-grandfather had retired from the army, he still looked every inch a general.

Gilbert might have been lonely in Paris at first if it had not been for his great-grandfather. The old gentleman told the boy exciting stories about battles in which he had fought. He took him on long walks to see the sights of the city.

Gilbert's mother had many social engagements and could not spend much time with him. It worried her because he had no playmates his own age. Soon she decided to send

He wished he were back at Chavaniac

him to a school for young noblemen. Since the school was in another part of Paris, Gilbert boarded there. But he came to see his mother often at the palace.

Gilbert had never been to school before. Yet Abbé Fayon had taught him so well that he was put in a class with boys his own age.

At first Gilbert was too shy to make friends. He blushed easily, and sometimes he stumbled over his own feet. He had a feeling that some of the boys looked down on him because he came from the country.

One day Gilbert's class had to write a composition describing a perfect horse. After class, the boys discussed what they had written.

"I wrote that a truly excellent horse is one which obeys his master's whip instantly," said young Louis de Noailles, a boy whom Gilbert greatly admired. "What did you write, Charles?"

"I wrote that a really perfect horse would obey when it was only threatened with a whip," replied Charles Fouchet. "It seems we all wrote just about the same thing."

[*20*]

"I didn't," said Gilbert. "I don't think a horse would be perfect if you could scare him with a whip. I wrote that the most excellent horse would be so high-spirited that if he were whipped he would throw his cruel master off his back."

"You'll catch it," said Charles. "Teachers don't want their pupils to write about rebelling against masters."

"I rather like what Gilbert said," remarked Louis de Noailles. And he looked at Gilbert in a much friendlier manner than he had before.

The next day the teacher talked to the class about the compositions. "They were very much alike," he said. "Only Gilbert's was different. He believes that a high-spirited animal cannot be mastered by force and cruelty. And it is my opinion, young gentlemen, that Gilbert is right. He has described the truly perfect horse."

Gilbert could not quite hide a pleased smile when he heard his composition so highly praised. And that same afternoon young Noailles asked Gilbert to practice fencing with him. By daring to write what he thought, Gilbert had made a friend.

A few days later Gilbert sat in his Latin class. The boy did well in Latin and he was studying hard when suddenly a quill pen whizzed by his left ear.

"Who threw that pen?" snapped Monsieur Everard, the Latin teacher.

There was a complete silence.

Monsieur Everard caught sight of Charles Fouchet. Charles was smiling and his dark eyes looked mischievous.

"Did you throw that quill, Fouchet?" cried the schoolmaster angrily.

"No, sir," Charles replied, grinning.

Striding across the room, the teacher grasped Charles by the arm and raised his cane. "I think you did," he cried, and he caned him soundly.

After Latin class, small groups of boys gathered together, talking angrily about the teacher's unfairness. They believed Charles even if the teacher did not. Nobody seemed to know where the quill had come from. But Charles was not to blame.

Gilbert was the most indignant of all the boys. "We must not stand for such treatment," he shouted excitedly. "We must rebel. When teachers are unjust, we must refuse to obey!"

"You'll get whipped if you go on talking like that," said one of his more timid classmates.

"I would resist a beating at the point of my sword," Gilbert yelled fiercely, just in time to be overheard by a passing teacher.

"You'll surely be in trouble now," said young Noailles. "It's all right to think like that, but you shouldn't shout about it. You'll be reported to the headmaster."

"All right! See if I care!" Gilbert cried.

But by now Gilbert did not feel nearly as defiant as he sounded. A few minutes later, he was sent for by the headmaster. He swaggered down the hall, so that the boys would not know that he was frightened.

The headmaster was a small, shriveled-looking man with bright, keen eyes. For some reason he was able to scare people who were twice his size. Now he seemed to look right through Gilbert.

[23]

"I understand that you're planning to start a rebellion here," he said gruffly to Gilbert.

Gilbert rubbed his sweating hands against his elegant green silk coat. "The Latin teacher punished Charles unjustly, sir," he said in a small voice. His fierceness had disappeared in the presence of the headmaster.

"I've heard the story," said the headmaster. "The teacher may have been hasty, but that's no excuse for your trying to start a rebellion against the whole school. Do you really think this is a bad school, Gilbert?"

"No, sir," Gilbert replied. "I guess it's usually a pretty good school."

The headmaster straightened his wig, which was slightly to one side. He opened a silver snuffbox and took a pinch of snuff. Then he said slowly, "Remember this. Never rebel against anything unless you're sure it's more evil than good. Do you understand?"

"Yes, sir," Gilbert replied meekly.

"Then see that you remember it. Another thing, Gilbert. Is it true you told the boys you'd use your sword on any teacher who tried to whip you? Answer me."

"I may have said something like that," Gilbert confessed.

"I'm surprised that a boy who intends to be a soldier should talk like that," said the headmaster. "You must know that if you become an officer in the army, you can't allow your men to rebel. In a school, the teachers are the officers. As long as you remain in this school, you must obey them."

When it was put that way Gilbert could see that his idea of starting a rebellion had not been a good one. "I understand," he said. But he still was not quite sure he could endure a whipping without fighting back.

"Stand up for your friends if you think they are unfairly treated, but learn to keep a cool head when you do so," said the headmaster. "That's all." And he smiled at the lanky red-haired boy.

"Did he beat you?" asked Gilbert's friend, Louis de Noailles, who was waiting just outside the headmaster's door.

"Of course not. He didn't lay a finger on me," boasted Gilbert. "Our headmaster hasn't a bad heart. He even has pretty good sense."

CHAPTER THREE

The Cadet

GILBERT sat opposite his great-grandfather and tried to eat his lunch. But it was of no use. He was too unhappy. For his beautiful mother and his grandfather had died within a few weeks of each other. At thirteen, Gilbert was now motherless as well as fatherless.

"I know you can't help grieving," said his great-grandfather. "But your sorrow will be easier to bear when you are back at school. Here, everything reminds you of your mother."

"I don't want to go back to school," protested Gilbert. "I want to go back to the country. Now that my mother is dead, I don't want to live in Paris."

THE CADET

"It was your mother's wish that you live in Paris," said the old general gently. "Now that I'm your guardian you must let me decide what is best for you. You must return to school. You will also begin your training as a cadet in the King's Black Musketeers."

"The Black Musketeers!" Gilbert looked pleased in spite of his sadness. For he knew that an appointment to that famous company of soldiers was a great honor.

The boys who belonged to that company came to school wearing marine-blue uniforms and orange caps. The hours of drill were usually after school. But on special days there were parades or inspections of the troop by the King. Then the cadets were excused from their classes.

"I've always wanted to belong to the King's Black Musketeers," said Gilbert. "I think my mother would want me to be a Musketeer."

"I'm sure she would," said his great-grandfather. "And I want to hear no more about your leaving Paris."

Soon Gilbert was busy again with Latin and

Greek. He was also learning how to be a soldier. Not a foot-soldier but a soldier on horseback, for the Black Musketeers rode sleek black horses.

Then came a proud day in Gilbert's life. King Louis XV was to inspect his troops on the parade ground outside his palace at Versailles. And Gilbert had been chosen to report to the King and to ask him if he had any orders for his Musketeers.

"I must ride up to the King alone and speak to him," he thought. "I will actually speak to one of the most powerful kings on earth."

When the Black Musketeers were lined up on the parade ground, Gilbert sat as tall as he could on his horse, Victor, and waited for the King to come from his palace.

A worried-looking officer rode up to give Gilbert his final instructions. But the boy already knew them as well as he knew his own name. His heart beat fast, however, when King Louis XV, with several attendants, rode onto the parade ground.

Now was the time for Gilbert to leave his

place in line and ride up to the King. For an instant he felt frozen in his saddle. Then he performed what he had rehearsed so many times. He rode up to the King, reined Victor to a stop, and saluted with drawn sword.

"Have you any orders, Sire, for the Black Musketeers?" he asked. He blushed as he realized that his sentence had begun in a shrill tone and had ended in a deep one because his voice had not finished changing.

The King's dull eyes in his puffy face hardly seemed to see the boy-soldier. "No orders," he said indifferently, and put up a fat hand, which was heavy with rings, to hide a yawn.

Now came the hardest part of all for Gilbert. He must back Victor at least twenty feet from the royal presence. The boy knew that every eye was on him. If he failed to keep Victor under perfect control he would be disgraced. But the horse seemed to know what was expected of him and behaved beautifully.

"Well done, though you sit your horse like a farmer," said Louis de Noailles, when Gilbert took his place in line beside him.

His heart beat fast when King Louis XV

rode out onto the parade ground

Gilbert beamed with pride. He was thankful that he had not fallen off his horse when he had saluted with his sword. He was thankful he had backed his horse correctly. He was thankful it was over.

Gilbert's company of cadets was dismissed after the inspection. He and Louis started back to Paris along the wide road on which the King's coach traveled between Versailles and Paris.

Gilbert kept thinking of the King. "He's so powerful he can send any man in this country to prison whenever he wants to. He can take away his property, too. He can even have him put to death," he thought.

He remembered hearing that the King had spent a great deal of money building new palaces and giving splendid parties at court. Indeed, King Louis XV had spent so much money that he had had to ask his subjects to pay very heavy taxes.

Gilbert knew that it was the poor people and not the nobles who paid these taxes. He had seen many pale, ragged people in the streets of Paris. He thought it must be hard

for the poor to pay taxes when
they did not have money
enough to buy bread
for their families.

Louis interrupted Gilbert's serious thoughts by riding close. "I'll race you into Paris from here," he shouted.

"All right!" Gilbert cried.

The two horses pounded along the dusty road, with Louis's horse in the lead. But neither Gilbert nor his horse, Victor, liked to be beaten. Gilbert did not need to use his spurs or whip to make Victor run like the wind. The horses were neck and neck when the boys reined them in at one of the gates that marked the entrance to Paris.

As they rode into the city, the Seine River sparkled in the sunshine like a glittering necklace. The carving on the front of a great cathedral looked like stiff gray lace.

"I think Victor came out just a nose ahead," said Gilbert.

"He did not. We both won," said Louis.

Later that day Gilbert and Louis went for a fencing lesson. While they sat in a bare room waiting for the slim, quick man who was their fencing teacher, Louis said, "What's this I hear about your being engaged to my cousin, Adrienne?"

"It's true," replied Gilbert with a smile. "But we aren't going to be married right away, you understand. Not until I'm sixteen."

"Her father and your great-grandfather arranged the marriage, of course," said Louis. "You will be one of the richest men in Paris. And Adrienne belongs to one of the most important families in France. Not that I mean to boast about my relatives."

"The marriage was arranged, as you say," said Gilbert. "But Adrienne and I have been allowed to get acquainted with each other. Some boys in France marry girls they hardly know by sight. But Adrienne and I are already friends."

"*En garde,* Marquis de Lafayette," snapped the crisp voice of the fencing teacher. And Gilbert quickly forgot everything except the joy of learning how to fence with skill.

CHAPTER FOUR

The Clumsy Courtier

THE walls of the ballroom in the Queen's palace, the Trianon, had panels of mirrors and of rose-colored brocade. Great crystal chandeliers glittered in the light from hundreds of flickering candles. Princes, dukes, and marquises bowed to their ladies in the stately figures of a dance.

Marie Antoinette, the Austrian princess who had married the heir to the French throne, was giving a ball. Now that old King Louis XV was dead, the young King and Queen held many parties at Versailles.

Gilbert was there, looking very elegant in a cloth-of-gold coat with lace ruffles at his throat. Between dances, he joined his friend, Louis de Noailles.

"There are always the same faces at the Queen's parties," Gilbert complained. "All noblemen but not all noble men, I'm afraid."

Louis smiled and asked Gilbert about his young wife. "Where's Adrienne tonight?"

"Adrienne wasn't feeling well enough to come," said Gilbert. "Let's leave early, Louis. I'm bored."

Just then a gentleman bowed to Gilbert. "The Queen requests the Marquis de Lafayette to be her partner in the next dance," he said.

Gilbert sighed, though he knew it was an honor to be chosen by the Queen. He crossed the room and bowed low before lovely Queen Marie Antoinette. She was dressed in pearly white silk tonight with diamonds in her hair.

It made Gilbert nervous to dance with the Queen. He made a misstep and Marie Antoinette remarked in her clear voice, "Your coat shows it was made in Paris, but your feet still belong in the country, Marquis de Lafayette."

It was an honor to dance with her

She laughed and people near by who had overheard her remark laughed too. Gilbert flushed. He thought that being a queen should not excuse a person for being rude. Suddenly it seemed to him that parties like this were a waste of time.

That night, riding home in the coach with Louis, Gilbert said, "I'm tired of going to the Queen's parties. I don't want to be a hanger-on at court all my life. I want to *do* something."

"Don't forget you're an officer in the King's Dragoons," Louis reminded him.

"I'm only a reserve officer at present. I won't be called to active service unless there's a war. And there is no war."

"There aren't any wars anywhere now unless you count the trouble England is having with her American colonies," said Louis.

"I've heard that the English have treated the American colonies most unfairly," said Gilbert. "I admire the Americans for revolting against England."

Louis laughed. He remembered the composition Gilbert had written at school about the excellent horse. "I see you still believe that the high-spirited horse should throw his cruel master off his back," he said.

"If the English are cruel masters, it's the duty of the Americans to revolt," insisted Gilbert. Then he changed the subject to less serious matters.

Gilbert thought a good deal and heard a good deal about America the next few months. One evening at a friend's house, he met a man named De Kalb. Baron De Kalb had been to America. He planned to return to the colonies and to serve in the American Army. Gilbert was interested in all that De Kalb could tell him about America.

"I've just about decided that I would like to help the Americans fight for their freedom from England," said Gilbert. "How does one go about joining the American Army?"

"Go and see Mr. Silas Deane, who is in charge of American affairs in Paris," De Kalb told him.

That night Gilbert broke the news to his family that he wanted to go to America.

[40]

*He was interested in all De Kalb could
tell him about America*

"Of all the boyish nonsense!" scolded his father-in-law. "I have been your guardian since your great-grandfather died, and you are only nineteen. Of course you can't go to America."

None the less, Gilbert went to call on Mr. Deane the next day.

Mr. Deane was pleased that such a rich young member of the French nobility wished to join the American Army.

"The only difficulty is that my father-in-law objects," said Gilbert. "But if I were to be given a high rank in the American Army he might change his mind."

"Just what rank in the American Army would you expect to hold?" asked Mr. Deane.

"That of major general," said Gilbert firmly.

"Nineteen is a bit young for a major general," said Mr. Deane doubtfully.

"But I doubt if I can go unless I hold that rank," Gilbert insisted.

"I'll see what I can do," promised Mr. Deane.

[42]

A few days later Gilbert went into his father-in-law's study and showed him a document. This document stated that the Marquis de Lafayette had been appointed major general in the American Army. The appointment, however, still had to be approved by the American Congress. Gilbert did not worry about having his appointment approved by Congress. In his mind he was already a general.

"It's ridiculous!" stormed his father-in-law. "No boy of nineteen can be a general. This document isn't worth the paper it's written on."

Gilbert snatched it out of the duke's hand. "I'm still determined to go to America," he said in an angry voice.

"Not if I can prevent it," said the duke grimly.

Soon Gilbert found another obstacle to his leaving for America. Mr. Deane suddenly advised him to give up going.

"I've received news from America that our army has had a crushing defeat. It looks as though we may not be able to win our freedom from England," said Mr. Deane worriedly. "And now your king has just issued orders that no ship can sail from France with arms and men for the United States. Thirteen French officers besides yourself are ready to sail for America and I can't get a ship to take them there."

Gilbert thought hard. By this time he had convinced himself that it was his duty to help the Americans. "I'll buy a ship to take us across the ocean," he said. "I can see that your country needs my help most in an hour of danger."

But young Lafayette soon found that a person could not buy a ship and set sail secretly for America without a good deal of scheming and planning. De Kalb helped him. He arranged for the purchase of a ship, which Gilbert renamed *La Victoire*. He decided also that Gilbert and the other French officers should sail from Spain since they might be stopped if they left from France.

Gilbert hated not being able to tell Adrienne about his plans. He hated to be obliged to leave home secretly. But he knew he would

He arranged for the purchase of a ship

have to leave secretly if he left at all. For the duke flew into a rage if Gilbert even mentioned America. And although the duke was a small man, he had a large temper.

A morning came when Gilbert was leaving home to visit England with Adrienne's uncle. Adrienne thought her young husband would be back in a few weeks. Gilbert knew he would be gone a long, long time. For he would not be coming home from England. He was planning to join his ship, which would be waiting for him in a Spanish port.

Gilbert longed to tell his wife everything. But he was afraid she could not keep a secret from her father. She was so gentle and her father so frightening when he was angry.

"Good-by, my dear." There was nothing more Gilbert dared say. A servant carried his luggage to the waiting coach.

Adrienne stood at the door and waved.

"She will be proud of me when I come back from America after winning many battles," Gilbert thought to himself.

CHAPTER FIVE

The Voyage

THE small ship, *La Victoire,* wallowed through a choppy sea. Down in his cabin, Gilbert was writing to Adrienne. He was telling her all he had longed to tell her before he left home. "If you are angry with me I shall be most unhappy," he wrote. "The long voyage across the Atlantic is tiresome."

There was a knock on his cabin door.

"Come in," said Gilbert.

"How's the seasickness, Marquis?" asked Edmond Brice, stooping to enter the low door. He was the only American on board and he was helping Gilbert learn to speak English.

"I no longer feed, what you say, the fishes," said Gilbert in halting English. "It is very difficult, your language. But I learn to speak her. I study hard. I make well, is it not so?"

"You're doing very well," Brice assured the young Frenchman. Though, to tell the truth, he found that Gilbert's English was still hard to understand.

"A wave," continued Gilbert, "is of the ocean. It is also what one makes with the hand to say good-by. Very, what you say, confusion. But liberty, ah, that is the word most like in French and in English. Also, *victoire* and victory. I am happy I understand those most beautiful words in your tongue."

"They are words I find beautiful, too," said Brice. The more he saw of this young French marquis, the better he liked him. And the two men became good friends before the voyage was over.

On June 13, 1777, *La Victoire* drew near the coast of South Carolina. Land looked good to Gilbert after fifty-four long days at sea.

The captain had hoped to sail into Charleston Harbor. In the distance, however, he saw two British frigates. He knew that if men on the British ships sighted *La Victoire* they might try to capture her. So he changed his course. Sailing quickly away from the frigates, he took his ship around a point of land and dropped anchor.

Gilbert was impatient to get ashore. He waited till after dark. Then he, Brice, and De Kalb slipped over the side of *La Victoire* and stepped into a small boat where two sturdy sailors waited to row them to land. There was no sign of a house on the bleak shore, so the sailors rowed the small boat up a river. Here black trees rose on either side of them, as their oars cut the dark water.

"Doesn't anybody live along this river?" asked De Kalb worriedly. "I'd hoped we'd find a place to spend the night. It must be close to midnight."

"What's that?" cried Gilbert, seeing a flickering light on the river.

"Make as little noise as you can," De Kalb told the sailors. Because he was older than Gilbert or young Brice, he was apt to take charge. "Row close to the light, but not too close."

The oarlocks creaked faintly, in spite of the sailors' effort to row silently.

[*49*]

"It's only two men in a boat out fishing by torchlight," said Brice, as they drew near.

"Where's the nearest house?" called De Kalb to the fishermen.

"Major Huger's house is round the next bend," one of the fishermen answered.

"I wonder what we will find round the bend," Gilbert thought, as the rowboat edged out and around and then in again toward shore. At last he saw the outline of a house not far from shore.

After the boat was moored, Gilbert and his companions approached the house. There was no sign of life until, roused by their approach, dogs inside set up a loud barking.

An upstairs window opened and a man leaned out. "Who's there?" he shouted.

"Friends."

"Who?"

"Gentlemen who have come from France to fight for America," De Kalb answered.

"I'll be right down."

The dogs stopped barking and the front door opened. Major Huger welcomed his unexpected guests with great kindness. He

Major Huger welcomed them kindly

called a servant to get them food and drink.

"Of course you'll stay all night," he told them, and ordered their beds made ready.

Gilbert slept well. When he woke up the next morning, the sun was shining. He looked out the window at tall trees and a sparkling river just beyond. "This America is a very pleasant country," he thought.

He went downstairs and met Mrs. Huger and her three-year-old son, Francis.

"Say 'Good morning, Marquis de Lafayette,'" said Mrs. Huger to the little boy.

The title and long name were too much for the small boy. But he tried. He returned Gilbert's smile with a pleased grin. Then he came and took Gilbert by the hand to lead him to the breakfast table.

"Usually Francis is shy with strangers. But he liked you at once," said Mrs. Huger.

"I am most happy that the son of a most gracious lady likes me," said Gilbert.

His English was still hard to understand, but his smile was so charming that Mrs. Huger liked him at once, too.

Gilbert stayed a few days with his new friends. Then he rode to Charleston, where *La Victoire* had made port after escaping from the British frigates. Soon he and the French officers who had crossed the Atlantic with him were on their way to Philadelphia.

Gilbert was in a hurry to present his papers to the American Congress and to have his appointment as a major general approved. He was sure that Congress would welcome him gratefully. They would realize that it had cost him a great deal to come to America. He was glad to make the sacrifice. But he soon began to wish that Philadelphia were not so far away from South Carolina.

The Frenchmen made most of the long journey on horseback. The roads were bad. The weather was sultry.

"Traveling like this is harder than fighting in a war," complained one of Gilbert's companions. "This country is too big, too wild. It's not civilized."

"It's a new country and I like it," said Gilbert. "Except for these horrible insects with bayonets," he added, slapping at a mosquito. "If the Americans knew how to train a regiment of them, and sent them against the British, they'd win a battle for the Americans."

The Frenchmen were on the road a weary month. At last, dusty and bone-tired, they reached the city of Philadelphia.

"It's not what I'd call a handsome city," said one of the officers.

Gilbert hardly heard him. He was rehearsing the words he would say to Congress. He would say, "I am happy to devote my life and my fortune to the American cause." Then he would probably have to wait while Congress cheered and applauded.

CHAPTER SIX

A Cool Welcome

IT WAS Sunday and Congress was not in session. Yet, hardly stopping to brush his coat, Gilbert was off to see John Hancock, the president of the Congress. Hancock sent him to another statesman, Robert Morris. And Morris agreed to meet Gilbert at noon the next day in front of Independence Hall.

Promptly at noon the next day, Gilbert and several other French officers paced up and down in front of the hall where Congress held its meetings. Ten minutes passed.

"In France," said one of the Frenchmen, "common people do not keep a marquis waiting."

"We have no need of your services at all"

"Remember, in America there are no common people," said Gilbert.

"Here he comes, and it's about time," complained another of the French officers.

Congressman Morris hurried toward the group of Frenchmen. There was another man with him.

"Good day, gentlemen," said Mr. Morris. "Mr. Lovell, here, has charge of dealing with all persons from your country. He speaks French. You may conduct your business with him." And Mr. Morris hurried on into the hall, leaving the Frenchmen standing on the sidewalk.

Without a word of greeting, Mr. Lovell began to scold Lafayette and his companions. "I don't know why you Frenchmen keep coming over here. Nobody asked you to come. You're not needed. Last year we could have used a few French officers. But not this year. We have no need of your services at all. Good day." And, without even a bow, he took his leave.

The Marquis de Lafayette had never in all his life been treated with such rudeness. He had expected a warm welcome from Congress. Instead, he was not even invited into the hall where Congress met.

He thought of the money he had spent in buying a ship. The sacrifices he had made in leaving his family. And now to be told he was not wanted! It was a bitter moment.

"These people are barbarians!" said one of the French officers.

And for once Gilbert did not speak up in defense of the Americans.

Gilbert was sad and worried that evening. He did not sleep well that night. For he knew that if he returned to France having accomplished nothing, he might be punished as well as laughed at. He had thought he would be forgiven in France if he won fame as an American general. But it seemed he was not wanted in America. He could not decide what to do.

The next day he had two callers, the rude Mr. Lovell and another man, Mr. Duer.

"What can I do for you, gentlemen?" Gilbert asked coldly, remembering the way he had been treated the day before.

"I've decided I may have spoken a mite hastily yesterday," apologized Mr. Lovell. "I had not then seen letters from Paris which spoke of you quite warmly."

"We've had trouble lately with a dishonest French officer who joined our army," said Mr. Duer. "But Congress now understands that you sincerely wish to help us."

"I was sure there had been some misunderstanding about me," said the young Marquis de Lafayette generously.

"Now, about your appointment as major general," said Mr. Duer pleasantly. "I'm not sure we can afford to pay another general."

"But I wish to serve without pay!" exclaimed Gilbert.

"Very generous of you," said Mr. Duer. "But would you be willing to serve under General George Washington with no troops of your own to command at first?"

Gilbert agreed to this somewhat unwillingly. He wrote a letter that evening to Congress, saying he would serve in the American Army without pay. He said also that he would

*"I wish the uniform could be ready
to wear to the dinner"*

begin his services as an honorary major general.

An afternoon two days later, Gilbert was in his room at the inn when Baron De Kalb came in.

"How goes it?" De Kalb asked. "I must say you're looking much more cheerful than you did a few days ago."

Gilbert's eyes shone. "I received my appointment as honorary major general this morning, and look what was delivered to me this afternoon!"

He opened a box and took out the sash of a major general in the American Army. "I must get measured for a general's uniform at once," he said, trying the sash on. "I wish the uniform could be ready for me to wear to the Union Tavern. I've been invited to a dinner there to meet General George Washington, who is now my commander in chief."

CHAPTER SEVEN

The Youngest General

THE Marquis de Lafayette dreamed he was in his luxurious home in Paris, sleeping on a bed of soft down. He woke up and found himself lying on a hard army cot in a tent which was pitched on the slope of a Pennsylvania hillside.

He shivered, for although he had slept in his uniform, the September air was chilly. But Lafayette did not even notice he was uncomfortable, because he was so happy to be in George Washington's army, learning the duties of a general.

How lucky he was, he thought, to have Washington for his commander in chief. He thought that Washington not only looked noble but was noble. He remembered the day Washington had begun to treat him as a friend.

Washington had invited him to inspect the American troops just outside the city of Philadelphia. Lafayette remembered how awkwardly the troops had drilled and how shabbily dressed they were.

"I suppose you find our army crude in comparison with French troops," Washington had said.

"I came here to learn, not to teach," Lafayette had replied.

He had seen that Washington was pleased with this answer. Now, Washington treated him almost like an adopted son. Lafayette was glad he had not told Washington that day what he had really thought of American troops. For now that he knew them, he liked the American soldiers. He knew they were brave men.

A bugle blew. Time to get up. Lafayette raised the flap of the tent. He could not see British soldiers, but he knew they were not many miles away.

[63]

*Washington had invited him to inspect
the American troops*

The Americans were camping near Brandy-wine Creek, not far from Philadelphia. Washington had told his officers that the British were planning to capture that city.

"If possible, we must keep the British from crossing Brandywine Creek," Washington had said. "We must be ready to fight them, even if we are outnumbered."

Now the Americans were waiting uneasily for the British to advance. All day long they waited. Shortly after daybreak the following morning they saw the British coming. At once they made ready to meet them in battle.

"Ride out with me to inspect our troops before they go into battle," Washington invited Lafayette. But to Lafayette's disappointment, the American leader said nothing about allowing him to take part in the fighting. And he could not fight unless General Washington permitted him to do so.

Lafayette spent most of the forenoon anxiously watching the fighting through field glasses. "If only there were fewer of the British and more of the Americans," he thought as he listened to the booming of the guns. As time went on, he grew more and more impatient to join the fighting.

Soon after noon he led his horse over to where General Washington stood.

"I've just heard that the British have managed to cross the Brandywine higher up the creek," said Washington. "General Sullivan is trying to hold them back, but he's hardpressed."

"Let me join General Sullivan's forces," begged Lafayette. "I came to this country to fight, not to stand still and watch. Do let me help."

Gravely, Washington gave his permission.

Lafayette sprang on his horse and galloped down the slope. He glowed with excitement, trembled with eagerness. Now he could smell the powder, see the guns flash. The dull boom of the cannon's roar was deafening. Suddenly he saw Sullivan's line break. American soldiers were running toward him in retreat. Soon they were all around him.

Lafayette jumped from his horse. He

Washington gave his permission

grabbed at a running soldier and spun him around. He struck at another with the flat of his sword. "Get back in your ranks and fight," he yelled at the top of his voice. *"En avant! Allez! Allez!"*

Young though he was, most of the soldiers obeyed his ringing voice and tone of command. They turned and followed him back into the battle.

"Shoot the redcoats down!" he shouted. *"Vive* George Washington! *Vive* America!" Again and again he urged the men on.

The British came forward like a rising tide. Wave after wave of redcoats surged about the Americans. The enemy was on all sides. But Lafayette would not retreat. He fought on. He fought until he felt a sudden weakness come over him.

"You're wounded, sir," cried his aide.

Lafayette staggered. He looked down and saw that his boot was full of blood. A musket ball had hit him in the leg. Suddenly his leg crumpled under him and he had to be helped to the rear.

[68]

"You're wounded, sir!" cried his aide

There his leg was bound up tightly with a scarf to stop the bleeding. Then Lafayette was taken to the town of Chester to have his wound dressed. He was placed gently on the dining-room table in a tavern. For it was thought that taking him upstairs to bed might start his wound to bleeding again. And he had lost too much blood already.

"What have we here?" cried the doctor, when he came to attend the wounded young man.

A smile lit up Lafayette's pale face. "I know I'm the only dish on the table. But don't eat me," he joked.

"I have orders from General Washington to care for you as if you were his son," said the doctor. "Now, I won't hurt you any more than I can help."

So, just a few days after his twentieth birthday, Lafayette had fought his first battle. He had shed his blood for his adopted country.

It was more than a month before Lafayette recovered enough to be able to rejoin Washington. Then, even though he still limped, he was eager to go into action again. In late November, he fought in the battle of Gloucester and conducted himself with great courage.

One day General Washington came to Lafayette with good news. "Marquis," he said, "today, I have received word that from now on you will be given a division to command. You are now a major general on active duty in the American Army."

"Good! Marvelous! Wonderful!" cried Lafayette. And he threw his arms about his dignified commander in chief and kissed him soundly on both cheeks.

"What conduct for a major general!" said Washington, laughing. "But *I'm* pleased, too. For in spite of your youth, Marquis, you possess uncommon military talents. I appreciate your loyalty and I respect your judgment."

Washington was not a man who praised anyone unless he really meant it. His youngest general was so pleased that for a moment he could not speak. Then he smiled. Yet there was a resolute look in his eyes.

"I am now fixed to your fate and I shall follow it and sustain it as well by my sword as by all means in my power," said Lafayette.

CHAPTER EIGHT

Lafayette and the Indians

LATE that autumn, Washington's army went into winter quarters at Valley Forge. There, Washington's youngest general took command of a division of troops from Virginia. And he learned the meaning of hardship.

"The log huts the soldiers have built to live in are hardly fit for cattle," he wrote to a friend in France. "Our army lacks uniforms, hats, shirts, and boots. Worst of all is the lack of food. The courage and patience of the soldiers seem a miracle to me."

Lafayette used his own money to buy food, blankets, and a few uniforms. But he did not have money enough on hand to feed and clothe

[72]

even his own division. He lived little better than his soldiers, and shared their discomforts. But he was always quick to smile and joke. His lightheartedness helped lift the spirits of the cold, hungry, and ragged soldiers.

"How goes it?" he would ask, as he made the rounds of the sentry posts at night.

"It's bitter cold," a shivering soldier would answer.

"It can't get much colder, so it must get warmer soon," Lafayette would say. And if a soldier seemed especially miserable, the young general might press a coin into his hand.

One frosty morning Lafayette was officer of the day. He had to receive reports and pass sentence on all soldiers who were reported for misconduct.

"Seth Babcock has lost his ramrod," a petty officer reported.

"Have him given five lashes." Lafayette hated to be so stern, but equipment was too valuable to be lost.

"Amos Finch has left camp. He has probably deserted."

[73]

"We can get along without fair-weather soldiers," snapped Lafayette. "Only weaklings leave when life in camp is hard."

"John Carter froze his feet. They had to be amputated."

"Poor fellow!" exclaimed the young general. "Tell him I'll come shortly to see what can be done for him."

"There is salt pork on hand for only one meal today. And the hardtack is nearly gone."

Lafayette reached in his pocket for a gold coin. "Buy a pig from a farmer with this," he ordered. "Surely, supplies purchased by Congress for the army must be on the way."

Later in the day Lafayette received word that Washington wished to see him. As they sat across a table, facing each other, Lafayette said, "I have just received a letter from France telling me that I have a baby girl. She was born soon after I left France."

"You must be homesick for your family and your country," said Washington kindly.

"As long as I feel that I am needed in America, I shall remain here," said Lafayette.

"We still need you," said Washington. "I have enjoyed having you under my command." He looked down at a paper in front of him. "I suppose it is no surprise to you, Marquis, that I have just received a message about you from Congress. You have been appointed by Congress to lead an expedition north to try to take Canada from the British."

"I had hoped for that appointment." Lafayette's eyes shone. "I don't mind the hardships here, but I want to *do* something, and not just sit in camp waiting for the winter to pass." He looked anxiously at Washington. "Don't you approve? Shan't I go?"

"You must make up your own mind, Marquis," replied Washington. And Lafayette was unable to tell if Washington approved of the expedition or not.

However, the idea of leading an army into Canada was an exciting one. The young marquis decided to go. Soon he and a party of officers were off for Albany, New York, on horseback. Lafayette was told that he would find three thousand men and military supplies waiting for him at Albany. His army was to be organized and equipped there before starting for Canada.

The February winds were cold and the roads were bad, yet Lafayette made good time to Albany. When he reached there, he did not find three thousand men waiting for him. He found only three hundred. As for military supplies, there were not enough to equip even that small company.

Lafayette was very much disappointed and very angry. "This is an outrage! Promises made to me have not been kept," he complained bitterly to General Schuyler, who was stationed at Albany. "I can't be expected to take Canada with only a handful of troops. I'd be a fool even to try. It couldn't be done."

"It would be madness," General Schuyler agreed.

"I shall return to General Washington at once," declared Lafayette.

"I wish you would go with me first up the Mohawk Valley," said General Schuyler. "The Iroquois Indians are holding a powwow there.

We want to persuade them to fight on the American side instead of the British."

Lafayette had never known any Indians. He was curious about them. He set off by sleigh with the group of Americans who were going to attend the powwow.

For two days the Americans and Lafayette sat for hour after hour around an Indian campfire. On the second day, General Schuyler made a long speech. The Indians listened, their faces without expression. The Americans presented gifts to them of beads, knives, and gunpowder. The Indians received these gifts. But they still would not agree to fight with Americans against the British.

Five hundred painted braves sat around the great bonfire on the third day. A new chief had just arrived. Like all the other Indians, he wore deerskin clothes and a feathered band around his black hair. But he was lighter in color than the others.

Lafayette took the pipe of peace from the light-skinned Indian chief. He puffed on it a few times, and passed it on to General Schuy-

They sat for hour after hour

around an Indian campfire

ler. "How long," he asked in French, "will it take these savages to make up their minds?"

The Indian chief overheard Lafayette's words. He smiled an un-Indian wide smile. "You French?" he asked Lafayette delightedly. "Long time ago, me French soldier!"

Immediately Lafayette and the light-skinned Indian chief were speaking French with each other. The man had been born in France, Lafayette learned. But he had lived with the Indians so long that he had almost forgotten he was French.

Soon Lafayette had made friends with a number of the Indians. They liked his pleasant ways and the gold coins he passed out. They would pierce holes in them and wear them around their necks, they told him.

At last the Indians agreed that they would fight on the American side.

"You certainly helped win them over," General Schuyler told Lafayette. "This has been a good afternoon's work."

"They wish to adopt me into their tribe," said Lafayette.

"Good," said the older man, his eyes twinkling.

The next day the ceremony took place by which the Iroquois Indians adopted the young Frenchman. They made him their brother, and gave him the name of a dead chief, Kayewla.

"We shall come to fight with you soon," some of the braves promised Lafayette.

But when Lafayette took his troops back from Albany to Valley Forge, no Indians rode with them. Perhaps they had never really intended to, Lafayette thought.

All the way back through the muddy roads of an early spring, Lafayette was dreading to report the failure of his Canadian expedition to Washington. Then, at last, he stood before his commander in chief. "I never do well when I'm away from you," he said humbly.

"It was an impossible undertaking. Whoever planned it, planned badly. You showed good judgment in giving it up," said Washington. "Now what's this I hear about your having become a brother to the Indians?"

[*81*]

"It's true," Lafayette said with a smile. "My Indian name is Kayewla."

A few days later a soldier ran to Lafayette. "A war party of Indians is advancing on us," he panted.

"Let them come," replied Lafayette calmly.

A party of Indians in full war paint came riding into camp. "We have come to help our brother, Kayewla, fight the British," said their chief.

Lafayette was so pleased that he embraced the first Indian who got off his horse.

One day not long after, Washington sent for his youngest general. "I need to know how many British troops there are across the Schuylkill River. Take a reconnoitering party of two thousand men and find out all you can."

Lafayette left camp with two thousand men, five cannon, and fifty Indian braves. He crossed the river. At nightfall he reached the village of Barren Hill, and camped there for the night. British troops moved up quietly in the dark. In the morning, Lafayette found his troops nearly encircled by redcoats. Thousands of redcoats.

"Looks like we're goners," said one soldier.

"I know a path that leads down to the river," said another. "Trouble is, we'd have to round a bluff in full sight of the British."

Lafayette spoke to the Indian braves. "Go into the woods beyond that bluff over there and make all the noise you can," he told them. "Shoot and yell and try to sound like a whole army. If the British think we have marched into the woods, they won't watch the bluff."

A few minutes later the woods rang with war whoops and musketfire. While the British advanced into the woods, Lafayette led his troops around the bluff and down the path to the river. They had forded it before the British realized that they had escaped.

Then the Indians came running out of the woods howling like wild beasts. The British dragoons were too frightened of the half-naked, screaming savages to shoot at them. The braves crashed through the underbrush to the river and dived in and swam to safety.

"The army across the river numbers more than eight thousand men," Lafayette reported to Washington. "And they were all after me."

"You showed good judgment and great skill," Washington praised him.

"The British haven't made the trap yet that will catch me," boasted Lafayette. "But I don't know how I would have come out this time without my Indians."

CHAPTER NINE

Lafayette Goes South

"THE only trouble with this war is that it's so long between battles," Lafayette complained to General Washington.

Washington smiled at his youngest general's impatience. After a year spent in France, Lafayette had rejoined Washington's army, which was now quartered near West Point in the State of New York. Now the two men sat across from each other at a table in Washington's crude log hut.

"You know it's not battles alone that win a war," Washington reminded Lafayette. "You were helping us all the time you were in France, by persuading your government to send us ships and troops, and money. And I haven't forgotten that you spent two hundred thousand dollars of your own money on our army when we were in desperate need. Your loyalty has helped me, too. You are brave in battles, Marquis, but you have helped just as much in other ways."

Lafayette put a hand on his sword. It was a beautiful weapon which had been presented to him by the American Congress in gratitude for his services to America. On the sword's hilt were pictures of the battles in which Lafayette had fought.

"But since I've been back in America, I've seen very little action," Lafayette complained. "I love the game of war. I want to *use* my sword."

Washington sighed. Then he gave Lafayette a look of deep affection. "I'm going to give you plenty of use for your sword this year," he said.

He unrolled a map. "British troops under General Phillips and General Arnold are just about overrunning this state," he said, pointing to Virginia. Then he slid his finger down the map a little way. "The English general—Cornwallis—is here in South Carolina with his army. My spies report that he is planning to march up to Virginia. If the British take Virginia they may march north.

"I can't give you men enough to defeat Cornwallis and his troops, but I want you to annoy them. Keep them busy. I'm putting you in charge of an army to march at once to Virginia. Can you leave by the end of the week?"

"Remember, the motto engraved on my sword means 'Why not?' " said the young general, his eyes shining.

Starting out at sunrise on a crisp, cold February day, Lafayette led a thousand men on a day's march of twenty-two miles. In a week he had marched them on foot a hundred miles through snow and slush and sleet and rain.

"We're nearly out of food," one soldier complained.

"We're out of medicine," said another.

"We have no carts and horses to carry the camp equipment," another man told Lafayette.

"The lighter we travel the quicker we'll get there," the general told his men. Yet he worried because he knew he did not have enough supplies of any kind.

At farms near Trenton he stopped to ask for food and carts for his soldiers. "Remember, it's your war, too," he told the farmers. Then, when his troops reached Philadelphia,

Lafayette persuaded Congress to give him money for shoes and medicine and a month's pay for his men.

Soon they were on the march again. As they went south, the soldiers began to grumble once more. They were nearly all northern

men, and had not been told they were going south. By the time they reached Maryland, in April, they were homesick and unhappy.

Lafayette camped his weary, ragged troops in Maryland near the town of Baltimore. He, too, was tired. And he was worried about the low spirits of his soldiers.

One morning after roll call he said to one of his aides, "Two men deserted yesterday. Four men left the day before. At this rate I soon won't have an army to take to Virginia."

"The men say the southern climate isn't healthy," said the aide. "And many of them want to get back home for their spring plowing."

"Those small-minded men who think more of their own fields than of their country!" stormed Lafayette. "I won't have men like that in my army. Call the troops together. I want to talk to them."

A half hour later Lafayette faced his men. It was a dank, damp day, and the soldiers looked as cheerless as the weather.

Lafayette talked to them kindly at first.

Then he spoke sternly. "Soon we will engage in one of the most important campaigns of the war," he told them. "You men are lucky to have the opportunity to do so much for your country. But I need *men,* strong, brave men. There is no room in my army for weaklings or for timid creatures who are scared to be away from home. I insist that all men of that sort leave this army at once.

"Yet I'll do this for the cowards who want to abandon me. You don't have to desert. I'll give any of you a pass that will let you rejoin the army in the north. Then here in the south we shall have left only men who are brave, resolute, and able to undergo hardship."

When he had finished speaking, Lafayette stalked back to his tent to wait for men to apply to him for passes. Not one man came. Instead, men who had deserted the day before, returned and tried to rejoin the army.

"You've made your choice," Lafayette told them. "I don't want wavering men who change their minds." And he made them start back north.

From that time on, the troops thought of being sent home as a disgrace.

Although he was sometimes stern, Lafayette had the needs of his soldiers very much at heart. They were barefooted and half-naked by this time, and he had no money for shoes and clothing. One day he went into town and borrowed money from the Baltimore storekeepers. He was able to borrow enough to buy stout overalls and boots. But the soldiers still had hardly a whole shirt among them.

One evening Lafayette was invited to attend a ball in Baltimore. The Baltimore ladies had heard a good deal about the gallant French marquis, and were eager to meet him.

In the ballroom that night Lafayette made courtly bows and pretty speeches.

"American women are quite as beautiful as the French," he said. "Especially the fair ladies of Baltimore."

While he danced stately minuets and quadrilles, he told his partners about his army, and about how badly his men needed shirts. "Any man who received a shirt sewed by your fair hands would treasure it," he said, not once but many times. Then he was pleased but not surprised when he learned that half the ladies of Baltimore were making shirts for his soldiers.

The ladies of Baltimore enjoyed Lafayette's company. So did the men. Young men from the best families of Maryland and Virginia rode out to his camp. They admired this young general who seemed to consider war an exciting game. Some of them joined his army. Soon Lafayette was commanding more soldiers than he had started with from New York.

One bright morning in mid-April, Lafayette and his army crossed the Potomac River into Virginia. Most of the soldiers were young. And every man among them was devoted to his young commander.

Around them, spring was coming into full bloom. The magnolias were fading but still filled the air with perfume. Cherry trees were in full flower. The soldiers broke sprays of cherry blossoms to wear in their hats. As they marched south, they saw purple blooms of wisteria hanging from white-pillared door-ways.

But the army had much grimmer busi-ness on hand than pick-ing flowers. The smell of gunpowder was stronger than the scent of flowering trees. La-

fayette hurried his men into Richmond just in time to prevent the city from being captured by the British.

A spell of hot weather set in.

"Massachusetts never has heat like this," a perspiring soldier named Henry Jones complained one morning to Lafayette.

"If you're too warm, cut off the bottom of your coat and you can move faster," joked Lafayette.

Henry Jones chuckled. Lafayette's good humor was catching. So was his gay courage. Later that day Henry walked beside his friend, Jed Bridges, as the troops moved cautiously through woods not far from the British lines.

"Funny, but I ain't scared of getting hit by a bullet when I'm following our young general," said Henry. "War seems almost fun. Of course the British have four times as many men as we have. But our general moves us around the country so fast they don't know how few we are, or what we're going to do next."

"I don't mind saying I was some worried when Cornwallis come up from Carolina and took charge of the British in Virginia," said Jed. "But our redheaded general's a match for him. Likely enough this afternoon we'll cut off a piece of the British Army, shoot them down, and then scoot off before the main army can catch us. Like playing hide and seek, it is. Sort of."

A trumpet sounded. "That means we start running again," said Henry. "Seems as if I've run over half the State of Virginny. Come on, Jed. Here we go again."

CHAPTER TEN

Cornering Cornwallis

D O YOU notice something different about us and the British lately?" Henry Jones asked Jed Bridges one sultry summer morning after roll call.

"Yup," said Jed. "First of the summer the British was chasing us all over Virginny. Now it's our troops doing the chasing. I guess our young general must have fooled Cornwallis into thinking we're at least twice as strong as we be. He's a smart critter, that young marquis of ours."

"He's mighty brave, too," said Henry. "I'll not forget the day he had two horses shot from under him. He ain't scared of nothing."

[*97*]

"What do you think he's up to now? Seems like we're chasing Cornwallis so close to Chesapeake Bay that he's liable to put his troops into ships and get away," said Jed.

Henry lowered his voice. "Where've you been that you haven't heard tell of the French fleet that's expected any day now? All we got to do is get Cornwallis cornered down here between the James and the York Rivers and then when the French fleet gets here— Well, I wouldn't want to be in the British general's shoes."

"How come you know so much about what's going on around here?" complained Jed.

"I keep my ears open when I'm cleaning the general's tent," said Henry. "Besides, General Lafayette don't try to keep secrets from his soldiers. Especially from me," he added smugly.

"You've been a-snooping and a-listening," Jed accused.

"Well, I always did enjoy knowing what was going on," acknowledged Henry. Then the two friends parted to go about their duties.

The oak trees in the southeast part of Virginia grew dry and dusty as the month of August drew near its close. Lafayette had chased Cornwallis into the town of Yorktown. Instead of moving on, Cornwallis had camped and was building strong fortifications.

Lafayette was worried. "If Cornwallis attacks us with his full forces, we'll have to retreat," he told one of his aides. "If I can only keep him cooped up until Admiral de Grasse gets here." He searched Chesapeake Bay through his field glasses. "Look!" he cried joyfully and passed the glasses to his aide. Soon, tall masts with white sails could be seen with the naked eye. The French fleet had arrived at last.

Lafayette went to call on the French admiral as soon as the fleet had anchored. He was rowed out to the flagship and visited the admiral in his cabin.

"You tell me that you are supposed to wait until Washington gets here before attacking Cornwallis," said Admiral de Grasse. "But why wait? I'll give you the help of my marines. It's only fair that you have the glory of defeating Cornwallis after fighting him for so long."

Lafayette did not speak for a long minute. He longed to do just what the admiral suggested. He thought that with the help of the admiral's men he would be strong enough to crush Cornwallis. But suppose he failed! "I'll have to think the matter over and let you know," he told Admiral de Grasse.

On his way back to camp, Lafayette stopped his horse in order to talk to an old man and an old woman and their grandson. The little boy was carrying a rooster under his arm.

"Cock-a-doodle doo!" crowed the rooster, drowning out Lafayette's friendly words.

"I can't make him stop crowing," said the small boy, looking ashamed of his pet rooster. "When I squeeze him he only crows the louder."

"Let him crow," cried Lafayette. "A crowing cock is a sign of good luck. He's crowing over our coming victory over the English."

He smiled and rode on. That crowing

[*100*]

rooster had helped him make his decision. He would not act without orders from Washington. Then he would be sure that the rooster would have something to crow about.

It was a happy day for Lafayette when he saw American and French troops under Washington's command come pouring into the countryside near Yorktown. He rode out to meet General Washington.

Washington greeted his youngest general warmly, and praised him. "The troops in Virginia could not have been in better hands," he said. "You have proved that you are an excellent leader."

Soon, an early frost had turned the tall oaks the color of rich blood. Starlings, on their way south, filled the air with a rusty clamor. Above them rose the noise of preparations for the siege of Yorktown. Trenches were dug. There was the heavy sound of cannon being placed in position. Danger held its breath while the British and the Americans prepared for battle.

Lafayette was in charge of two brigades on the right wing of the American Army. Beside his ragged American troops the French soldiers looked smart in their fine uniforms. "Are your men soldiers? How do they fight?" a French officer asked Lafayette.

"They fight like heroes," boasted Lafayette.

He was soon to put them to the test. Orders came that he was to attack one of the two British outer fortifications. The French troops were to attack the other. Huddled with his men in a trench, Lafayette gave his orders.

"Fix bayonets. Aim. Fire. Charge!"

The men sprang from the trench and stormed the British fortification so quickly that they took the redcoats by surprise. They captured the fortification while the French were still fighting. It pleased Lafayette very much to offer to send American soldiers to help the French, even though they were not needed.

The siege went on. Boom! Boom! Boom! The American cannons spoke and the British cannons answered. Day after day. Week after week. Smoke hung heavy in the air.

"We're a-gaining on them," boasted Henry Jones to Jed Bridges when they had been ordered to abandon their trench and dig another nearer the British lines.

A day came when firing from the British

"Fix bayonets. Aim. Fire.

Charge!'' Lafayette ordered

guns grew weak. "We're closing in on them," gloated Henry Jones. "Listen!" he ordered his friend Jed. Every British gun was silent but they could hear a drum beating. And they saw a British drummer perched on a barricade.

"Hip hooray! That means a truce," cried Henry, just as two British soldiers holding a white flag approached the American lines.

Cornwallis had been defeated at last!

The terms of surrender were signed at noon October nineteenth, but the ceremony of surrender did not begin till two o'clock. Lafayette stood with his troops watching the British walk through the American lines. Their band was playing a tune called "The World Turned Upside Down," and Lafayette thought that must be just the way the British soldiers were feeling.

The British soldiers kept their eyes turned away from the Americans, as if they could not bear to look at them. "Go tell *our* band to play 'Yankee Doodle,'" Lafayette told Henry Jones. And when the band blared "Yankee

Doodle," the British soldiers looked toward the American lines.

Lafayette watched the British soldiers lay down their arms and surrender their flags. "This is a sight that was worth waiting for," he said happily. "After this, what British general will dare try to conquer America?"

Now that Lafayette felt sure that the war would be won by the Americans, he wanted to return to France.

"Good-by," he told his loyal troops. "You are brave fellows and I love you all. And I love my adopted country, America. But my help is no longer needed here, so I must go home to my family in France."

"He's pretty young to be so much of a hero," said Jed Bridges to Henry Jones, the day Lafayette started on his way to France.

"Yup, he's young," agreed Henry. "He's only twenty-four but he's accomplished more already than most folks do in a lifetime. We won't forget our young marquis easy, here in America." And Henry had to wipe a speck of dust from his eye.

[*107*]

CHAPTER ELEVEN

The People's Friend

A LITTLE to the right. There. That's perfect." Lafayette was watching a servant hang two picture frames on a wall of his Paris home.

His eight-year-old daughter, Anastasie, came into the room and stood beside her father. "Where are the pictures?" she asked. "Why, one frame doesn't have anything in it at all."

"These frames are not meant for pictures, my dear," her father explained. "See the writing in the one to the right? That is a copy of America's Declaration of Independence. I told you about that, remember? It tells why people have a right to be free. The other frame

"Where are the pictures?" she asked

will stay empty until there is a declaration of the rights of the French people to put in it."

Little Anastasie slipped her hand into his. Her father was always talking about how much freedom people had in America and how little freedom people had here in France. She was not old enough to understand why this was so important. But she knew it must be, if her father said so.

She did not, however, quite believe him when he said that George Washington was the greatest man in the world. She often looked at Washington's portrait, which hung in her father's study. But she thought her father was just as great. Why, since he had come back a hero from America, people in the streets often cheered him as he passed.

"*Vive* Lafayette!" they would shout.

The Lafayettes were a family of five now. Anastasie's five-year-old brother was named for George Washington. And the baby was called Virginie, after the state of Virginia. A famous American statesman, Benjamin Franklin, wrote to Lafayette, "I hope you will have a child to name after every state in the union. Only perhaps Connecticut would be too awkward a name for a little girl."

Since the marquis had returned to France, he often invited American guests to his home to dinner. He especially enjoyed talking to Thomas Jefferson, an important American who was at that time in France.

One night Lafayette served his guests some cheese cut from a five-hundred-pound cheese. This giant cheese was a gift from America. It was from the whalers of Nantucket. They were grateful to Lafayette because he had persuaded the French Government to encourage trade in whale oil with America. Each man of Nantucket had given one day's milk from a cow to make this giant cheese for Lafayette.

"Excellent cheese," said Mr. Jefferson, tasting it.

"Most things from America are of great excellence," remarked Lafayette. Then his face looked very serious. "Especially your government," he said. "More than anything in the world I would like to see a government in

[*111*]

This cheese was a gift from America

France very much like yours in America."

That was Lafayette's dream, to make over the government of France. He could see the need for many changes in the French Government. The expenses of the King and the court were getting higher and higher, while most of the people were growing poorer and poorer. There was great poverty and suffering among them. Yet there was talk of taxing the people even more heavily. Lafayette thought that this was most unfair.

One day he had a chance to state this in public. The Government of France was greatly in debt. So the King had called a meeting of the nobles to discuss ways of raising some money.

"It's simple. Just make the people pay higher taxes," suggested an old duke, as he straightened the fine lace ruffles above his embroidered waistcoat.

"The poor will starve if they have to pay heavier taxes," declared Lafayette. "Too much of what they have already paid has been wasted. Why should people go cold and hungry so that the fountains can play for the King at Versailles? I tell you the people are growing rebellious because of the waste and extravagance at court."

King Louis XVI and Queen Marie Antoinette were angry when they heard that Lafayette had complained because they were extravagant. They were angrier still when they learned that Lafayette was talking to many people about the need for changing the French Government. And they were furious with him when he demanded that people from all parts of France should be allowed to send representatives to a National Assembly in Paris.

One evening Lafayette glanced up from a letter he was writing. His wife's face, bent over her embroidery, looked worried, he thought.

"Do you mind, my dear," he asked, "that we aren't invited to court any more?"

"Not at all," she said. "But it worries me, Gilbert, to hear that the King and the Queen are so angry with you."

"You can't really blame them," said Lafayette. "The King is rather a dull fellow. But
he's smart enough to know that I'm working
to take away most of his powers and give them
to the people. It's a change that has to come.
But naturally it will take the King some time
to get used to reforms in the government."

Adrienne sighed. "I worry for fear that any
day the King will have you arrested and flung
into the Bastille."

"A time will soon come when the King
won't have the power to send any man to that
grim old prison without a trial," said Lafayette. "I tell you, better days are coming for
the French people!"

"I hope so," said Adrienne. But she still
was worried about her husband's safety.
"Countess de Brienne says her husband is
angry with you because you said that the
nobles as well as the common people should
pay taxes," she said.

"I did say that. I feel strongly that the nobles should be made to pay their share. And I
don't believe that any king should have the

[*115*]

power to tax his people without their consent," said Lafayette earnestly.

"I'm sure whatever you think is right," said Adrienne gently. But she still looked worried.

"Louis XVI is not as bad as the two kings who ruled before him," said Lafayette. "But he must be made to see that times have changed. The people are demanding the right to help govern their country. They are insisting on choosing men to help make the laws. If the King refuses to let them do so, I'm afraid there'll be grave trouble."

"I hope there'll be no bloodshed," said Adrienne.

Lafayette hoped, too, that the King would give up some of his power without being forced to do so. He was pleased when Louis XVI at last agreed to let the people choose representatives to meet in a National Assembly.

These representatives met to discuss how France should be governed. They held their meetings in a hall at Versailles. But the King soon found out that they were planning to

Lafayette read the Bill of Rights

write a Constitution that would take away most of his powers. So he tried to keep them from meeting by ordering the doors of the hall locked.

"It will take more than locking us out of a meeting place to keep us from working together," cried one of the men angrily.

"Don't go home, gentlemen. The King can't break up our assembly. We'll find another hall," shouted a tall man dressed in somber black.

Shortly afterward, the men surged into an enclosed tennis court. They sat on hard benches overlooking the courts. They decided not to run the risk of being locked out of a meeting place again.

"We will stay where we are day and night until we have written a new set of laws to govern France," they declared. "Unless the King sends an army against us, he cannot stop us."

Lafayette had already written out a Bill of Rights. He read it to the Assembly. Then he and other men wrote new laws. There was much arguing over these laws. But, little by little, a Constitution was being drawn up. By its laws, the King would still be King. But he would have less power than that of a President of the United States. For the people of France were no longer willing to be ruled by kings.

One hot July night, Lafayette slept badly on his hard bench in the tennis court. He kept waking up and lying awake to think.

"Drawing up a Constitution for France is harder than fighting on a battlefield, and just about as dangerous," he thought. "But I'm proud to be doing it."

Then he remembered the rumors he had been hearing about how impatient the people of Paris were getting. They wanted new laws at once. The Assembly was not working fast enough to suit them.

"It will take time for the people to learn to use their freedom wisely," Lafayette thought. "They have been held down too long."

The next morning, Lafayette's friend, Louis de Noailles, hurried up to Lafayette. He was flushed and out of breath. "Have you

[119]

"The mob went in

like tigers"

heard?" he cried. "I've ridden hard from Paris to tell you the news."

"Heard what?" Lafayette wanted to know.

"The Bastille!" panted Louis. "A mob of people tore it apart." He drew a breath. "Last night," he gasped.

"Tore apart the prison?" Lafayette asked in amazement. "No! They couldn't."

"Couldn't? They did. Listen, Gilbert. Somehow the mob got guns. I heard noise in the street. Something like people running to a fire. Only they had guns, knives, pikes, clubs; any weapon they could lay their hands on."

"But they couldn't get to the Bastille!" Lafayette exclaimed. "What about the drawbridge over the moat? Wasn't that up?"

"Of course it was up. But a man cut the chain and lowered it. Then the mob went in like tigers. It was awful, Gilbert. They went completely wild. They hacked the guards to pieces. They hanged the governor of the prison. They set the prisoners free. The poor prisoners acted as if they were scared to death of the men who freed them."

[122]

"Poor souls—buried alive in that dreadful place for so long," said Lafayette. "It must never again be possible in France to send a man to prison without giving him a fair trial."

"But it was a dreadful riot, Gilbert," said Louis.

"Riot? It's Revolution!" cried Lafayette. "I tell you, July 14, 1789, will be a day long remembered in France. The day the Bastille fell. The day that hateful symbol of tyranny was destroyed. I'm sorry there was bloodshed. But you can't make an omelet without breaking eggs. After this, nobody, not even the King, can keep the people from getting their just rights."

CHAPTER TWELVE

The March to Versailles

An ANGRY mob surrounded an elegantly dressed old nobleman, who was just getting into his carriage.

"String him up to a lamppost!" bawled one of the men in the crowd.

"Cut off his head and I'll carry it around on a pole to show what we do to dirty aristocrats!" yelled another.

"Stuff his mouth with hay. He and his like starved my little girl. We had no bread for the poor puny child," muttered a thin man with long, uncombed dark hair.

Arms reached out to seize the terrified old gentleman. A tall thin woman snatched off the old man's wig and put it on her own head. The old man was as bald as a baby and just as help-less. "Help! Help!" he squeaked.

There was the quick sound of horses' hoofs. Down the street came Lafayette riding a white horse.

"What's going on here?" he shouted.

When the men saw him, they let the old gentleman go. He darted into his carriage like a mouse seeking its hole. He did not even stop to get his wig back.

"Citizens," cried Lafayette in a ringing voice, "to have hanged a defenseless old man would have been a poor use to make of free-dom. You should be ashamed of yourselves. Nobody has worked harder than I have for liberty. But as commander of your National Guard it is my duty to preserve order in Paris. Which I intend to do—with your help."

"*Vive* Lafayette, the people's friend!" yelled somebody.

"*Vive* Lafayette!" the crowd roared.

Lafayette rode away to the sound of these cheers. But he was troubled. He had been put in command of an army of citizens called the

National Guard, which was to keep order in Paris. But this was not easy to do. Since the fall of the Bastille there had often been dreadful fighting in the streets between the people who wished freedom for France and those who sided with the King. Lafayette could always stop such violence. But he could not be everywhere at once. Men *had* been hanged from lampposts.

Lafayette knew that one reason the people of Paris were so quick to make trouble was because they did not have enough food. The price of bread had gone up. Sometimes there was no bread to be bought at any price. And bread was the chief food of the poor.

This morning, as he rode toward his headquarters at the City Hall, Lafayette noticed that bakery after bakery had closed shutters. Usually by this time in the morning people would be coming out of the bakeshops with long loaves of bread under their arms. It did not seem possible that so many shops were without bread.

Lafayette dismounted, tied his horse, and

knocked at a bakery door. After he had knocked several times, a bleary-eyed man opened the door. The baker's face was as pasty-white as the flour he usually made into bread.

"Why is your store closed?" Lafayette asked.

"I have no flour. No grain is coming into Paris," said the baker sullenly. "It's the Queen's fault. She means to starve us. Everybody knows she's plotting with her relatives in Austria. She wants them to send troops into France to restore her husband's power. She's a wicked one, Queen Marie Antoinette!"

"As soon as the new Constitution becomes the law of the land," said Lafayette earnestly, "the King will have to swear to support it. Then if the Queen is plotting with the Austrians, she will have to stop it."

"I don't trust either of them," muttered the baker.

"What's that?" asked Lafayette suddenly, for he heard shouting and running in the street beyond.

[*127*]

Even as he spoke, a horde of women surged into the street of the closed bakeries. Hundreds of women with streaming hair and wild, excited eyes. They carried kitchen knives, axes, clubs. From where he stood, Lafayette heard a hoarse sound of voices, like the waves of an angry sea.

"You can't stop them," shouted the baker, pushing his red, angry face close to Lafayette's. "The women of Paris are marching to the palace in Versailles. My wife's with them. They are going to demand that the King and and Queen give them bread. I hope they cut out the Queen's heart."

"Wild talk like that does no good," cried Lafayette, mounting his white horse. He rode quickly to the headquarters of the National Guard and called out the troops.

"We must ride to Versailles," Lafayette told his men. "We'll not hinder the women from marching there. But we'll be on hand to prevent disorder."

It was a drizzly October day with a chill in the air. Before they had gone far on their way

[*128*]

to Versailles, the women were plodding along the road instead of running.

Lafayette stopped to talk to some of them. He told them it might be a good idea to send representatives into the palace to tell the King and Queen how badly the people of Paris needed bread.

"Appoint three or four of your number to enter the palace and talk to the King," he said.

The women listened to him. They were calmer by now. A few of them hid their knives, or threw down their clubs. They were citizens laying a just complaint before the King, they decided. The anger of the mob grew less.

Some of the skirted figures among them, however, kept out of Lafayette's way. Now and then he caught sight of men's trousers under the skirts. He realized that these men who were disguised as women were up to no good.

There was, Lafayette knew, a group of men called Jacobins who were working as hard to stir up trouble among the people as he was working to prevent it. For they wanted a bloody Revolution, not an orderly one. They wanted to seize power and rule the country themselves. Lafayette knew that there were Jacobins among the marchers today.

Yet when the mob reached Versailles, the

women followed Lafayette's advice. They chose representatives from their number to go into the palace to see the King.

These representatives came back reporting that the King had received them kindly. He

had promised to have more bread in Paris. He
had even promised to have all the loaves of
bread in his palace distributed to the people.

Lafayette had hoped that the women would

return to Paris after having talked to the King.
Instead, they camped near the palace. They
built bonfires in order to keep warm. They
sang loud songs, and made speeches. At last
they quieted down and slept.

Lafayette now tried to get a few hours' rest himself. He slept until dawn. Then he woke suddenly. One of his guards was shouting at him.

"Wake up, General Lafayette," the guard cried excitedly. "They're breaking into the palace. The mob is going after the Queen. They'll murder the King and Queen in their beds, unless you stop them."

Lafayette hurried his armed men to the palace grounds. He was sure the Jacobins had started this trouble.

Screaming women stood under the palace windows, howling insults at the Queen. Bang! Bang! Crash! That was the sound of men battering down locked doors. Now an outside door was down and a horde of people streamed in. They roared like wild beasts.

Lafayette and his men hurried into the palace. They saw old hags stop to stare at the beautiful wall paintings and gorgeous tapestries. Glass tinkled as one woman broke the door of a richly carved cabinet. She grabbed a pretty little snuffbox. Other arms reached out.

In three seconds the cabinet was empty of its small treasures.

Some of the mob were running upstairs to the Queen's rooms. Lafayette and his men ran upstairs by another staircase. He saw the Queen hurrying with her children into the King's rooms. The mob was not yet there. Screams of pain rose above the angry shouts of the people.

Lafayette rushed into the King's room.

"They've killed several of your bodyguard, Sire," he cried. "Why didn't your bodyguard resist them?"

"I told them not to fire on the people," said the King. "I didn't want anybody to be hurt."

"Sometimes force has to be met with force," said Lafayette, drawing his sword. And when the mob tried to enter the King's quarters, they were met by Lafayette and his armed troops.

The mob lost courage when they saw drawn swords and guns. Soon the palace was cleared. But the mob still stood outside. They still yelled threats against the Queen.

[*133*]

"Madame," said Lafayette to the Queen, "I think the best way to quiet them is for you to go out on the balcony and show yourself to the people. That will take courage, and the French people admire courage."

Marie Antoinette looked coldly at Lafayette. She hated him. She blamed him more than she blamed anybody else for the loss of power the King had been forced to accept. But she would not show fear before him. She stepped out on the balcony with Lafayette. Her beautiful, proud face seemed unmoved by the howls and jeers that greeted her.

Lafayette realized that her courage had not won over the people. Nor were they in a mood to listen if *he* spoke to them.

"But the people know that I am their friend," he thought. "Perhaps it will help if I show that I still respect the Queen." So he knelt and kissed her hand.

Something about his act pleased the people. They stopped screaming insults and began to shout:

"Long live the King! Long live the Queen!"

[*134*]

Lafayette sighed with relief. Even the Jacobins would not be able to stir up the mob again today, he knew. He went down to the courtyard to tell the people to go home.

They replied that they were ready to go, if

the King and Queen would go back to Paris too. Lafayette could not blame them for insisting upon this. Paris was the center of the French Government, and the King really belonged there.

As they neared Paris,

it seemed sad

"It is necessary that you live in Paris until conditions are more settled," Lafayette told the King and Queen.

"I suppose we have no choice but to obey," said the Queen.

"You will be wise to move to Paris," advised Lafayette.

The Queen looked at him haughtily. "I would have preferred to die today than to have been saved by the Marquis de Lafayette."

Later, riding beside the royal coach on the way to Paris, Lafayette felt far from cheerful. He knew that the Queen hated him because he had started the revolt of the people against the King. And he was beginning to see that the Jacobins also hated him, because he wanted to preserve law and order.

"If only I can make the King accept the Constitution and stop plotting to regain his power," he thought. "If only I can make the people see that liberty through law is the only freedom that will endure."

As they neared Paris, it seemed to Lafayette sad and cheerless under a sullen sky.

CHAPTER THIRTEEN

France Turns Against Her Best Friend

M AY I pat Jean Leblanc?" asked a small boy just as Lafayette was about to mount his white horse.

"Yes. He likes to be patted," said Lafayette. He was always kind to small boys.

"Is it true that your horse smiles and paws with his hoofs when people cheer for you?" the boy wanted to know.

"Perhaps. Jean Leblanc is my true friend. Though, to tell the truth, I've never caught him smiling. Are you going to the celebration at the Champ-de-Mars today, my boy?"

"Of course. My mother may stay at home because it rains, but bad weather will not keep my father and me away. I shall wear my tri-

"It's a badge to wear proudly"

color cockade on my cap. But until I get there I'm keeping it dry under my coat."

He showed Lafayette a perky blue, white, and red cockade. All people who supported or pretended to support the Revolution, wore tricolor cockades.

"It's a badge to wear proudly," said Lafayette, mounting his horse. "It shows the colors of a free France." Then he waved to the small boy as Jean Leblanc was off at a gallop.

As he rode out to the Champ-de-Mars, a plain on the edge of Paris, Lafayette wished that the drizzle would stop and the sky would clear. For today Paris was celebrating the first anniversary of the taking of that great prison, the Bastille.

Lafayette had arranged that on this day the King would take an oath to support the Constitution. He wanted all the people in Paris to be there to see the King publicly accept laws that would make France a free country. To be sure, the Constitution was not finished. But Bastille Day was the proper time for the King to pledge his support of the new government.

Men had been at work for days building an outdoor theater at the Champ-de-Mars, with tiers of seats all around it and an altar in the center. Lafayette sat on his white horse and watched people stream into the theater. Their clothing was damp, but they were cheerful.

He saw the King take his place on a throne, and the Queen and her attendants take their seats in a box. Flags waved in the breeze. Everything was gay in spite of the showery weather.

Lafayette rode to the altar and reined in his horse.

"*Vive* Lafayette!" the people shouted. They stamped and yelled.

"See Lafayette on his white horse go galloping down the ages," one man said to another.

There was a short religious service at the altar. Then Lafayette drew his sword and held it high. That was the signal for the members of the National Assembly to rise. Standing proudly, they swore their loyalty to the King and to the Constitution.

Lafayette waved his sword again and the

He swore to accept the Constitution

King rose. Before all Paris, he swore to accept the Constitution and to support it.

Then Lafayette dismounted. He went to the altar, laid his sword down, and took his oath of loyalty to King and Constitution.

Flags were unfurled and all the people in the stands rose and swore to support the new government. Cannon roared in loud salute to freedom. The clouds rolled away and the sun came out and shone upon people dancing and singing as they celebrated their new freedom.

People thronged around Lafayette and his white horse. "He is the French George Washington. He has brought freedom to us. He's the people's friend," they said. A small girl actually kissed Jean Leblanc. Lafayette's horse must have been pleased with all the applause his master received that day.

Lafayette hoped that a democratic government for France had at last been established. According to the new Constitution, the King would still be the head of the government. But the power to tax and to make laws would now be in the hands of the people.

It was not long, however, before the King

showed he had not meant to keep his solemn oath to accept the Constitution. He broke promises. There were rumors that he and the Queen were still plotting with the Austrians.

Many nobles had fled from France and joined the Austrian Army. Now that army was just beyond the French frontier. The French people expected that at any minute the Austrians might invade France and try to restore the King and the nobles to power.

One night the King and Queen tried to escape to Austria to join the others who had fled from France. Lafayette gave orders to have them arrested and brought back to Paris. Because they had failed to escape, the King and Queen hated Lafayette more than ever.

The Jacobins hated him even worse. While he remained so popular with the French people the Jacobins could not grab power and rule the country as they wished to. They told wicked lies about Lafayette, and stirred up all the trouble they could. Lafayette had to go about Paris trying to keep order, but not always succeeding.

One day he came home looking more cheerful than he had for some time. "Get the servants to pack," he told Adrienne. "We're leaving for Chavaniac in the morning. The Constitution is finished, and I've resigned from the National Guard. They can get along without me now."

Chavaniac seemed restful after Paris. Lafayette had time to play with his children. One afternoon he showed them where he had hunted the wild beast of the forest. But when he and the children returned to the château, Lafayette found a messenger waiting for him.

Lafayette's face was grave when he had read the message. "I have to leave at once," he told his family. "War has begun between Austria and France. I must go to take command of an army on the frontier."

It seemed to Lafayette like the old days in America, now that he was in command of an army once more. It took him some time to get the army properly organized. And before he could lead his troops into battle, he received dreadful news from Paris.

His enemies, the Jacobins, had gained control of the French Government! And they were determined to get rid of Lafayette!

It was not long before he received a message from Paris dismissing him from his army command. He was also ordered to return to Paris to be tried for being disloyal to the French Government.

"They accuse me, the best friend of freedom France ever had, of being a traitor," Lafayette said bitterly to one of his loyal officers. "If I go back to Paris the Jacobins will put me to death. And that will not help my country. I shall leave France at once, so that I may live to fight again for freedom."

Hurriedly, Lafayette wrote to Adrienne, telling her he must flee from France. He left orders with his army telling them what they should do in case they were attacked by the Austrians. Then he and several officers who insisted upon going with him crossed the frontier into Austria. They were on their way to Holland, where they would be safe.

It was a sultry August day. The Frenchmen rode rapidly, hoping to get to Holland with-

They had hoped to reach Holland

out being stopped. But their luck failed them.

"Halt!" cried an Austrian soldier.

Quickly the Frenchmen were surrounded by soldiers. They were taken before an Austrian officer.

Lafayette explained to the officer that he and his companions were no longer fighting for France. He explained also that they were on their way into Holland, which was a neutral country.

At last he convinced the officer that he was speaking the truth.

"If you will give me information about the French forces, I will let you go on," said the officer.

But Lafayette was too loyal a Frenchman to do that, no matter how badly his country had treated him.

Then the Austrian officer angrily ordered Lafayette and his companions to be put under guard, and taken to prison. Lafayette was told that he was being put into prison because he was the most dangerous enemy on earth to kings.

CHAPTER FOURTEEN

The Prisoner

FEEBLE light came through the one barred window of a dismal cell. There was never sun enough to dry the damp that oozed from the stone walls. A foul smell from an open sewer just outside the prison filled the air. This gloomy cell was in the Austrian fortress of Olmütz. And the thin, ragged man who sat shivering on his straw bed was Lafayette.

Far down the corridor he heard keys turn in rusty locks. One after another, four doors creaked open. Two armed guards entered the cell. One brought an earthenware bowl containing the prisoner's dinner. This was a greasy stew, filled with lumps of stringy meat. Since Lafayette had no knife or fork, he had to eat with a pewter spoon or with his fingers.

"It must seem strange for a man like you, who is used to fine living, to eat with your fingers," mocked the guard.

"I've seen it done among the Iroquois Indians," said Lafayette. His voice was hoarse.

"It sounds rusty from lack of use," he thought to himself.

Weeks went by when nobody spoke a word to him or he to anyone.

Except for his jailors, he was always alone. Once in a while he was given a book to read. One day he tore a blank page from the front of a book and wrote a letter. He used a quill toothpick for a pen and mixed soot with vinegar for ink. Usually he was too closely guarded to dare to write.

He had spent more than two years in solitary confinement in prison. A weaker man would have lost his mind. Or he might have tried to kill himself.

Not Lafayette.

"Don't worry. I won't oblige you by killing myself," he told his Austrian guards.

But his body was not as strong as his spirit. He had grown very thin. Now he coughed a great deal, and suffered from fever and chills. At last he became so ill that the governor of the prison sent a doctor to see him.

"I have heard a great deal about you, sir," said the doctor, who was a plump, pink-faced man.

"I did not realize that Number 812 was known outside these walls," Lafayette replied feebly. In prison he was called only by this number. He had been told that his name would be forgotten.

"I am not the only one who knows that Number 812 is the Marquis de Lafayette," said the doctor in a low voice.

Lafayette did not answer. He felt too ill.

The doctor clasped his hands over his fat stomach. "Like you, I am a great admirer of the United States and of George Washington," he said, with a quick look at the near-by guard.

Life seemed to come back into the sick man's dull eyes. "He was my beloved general,"

[152]

he said gently. Then his eyes sought the doctor's. "Perhaps you are not like the others here. Perhaps you can tell me what has happened to my wife and children. The jailors keep everything from me. Tell me what is going on in France."

"I can tell you nothing," said the doctor in a loud voice. "I come only to give you medical attention. Now I will take your pulse." Then, as he held Lafayette's thin wrist, he whispered, "You have friends outside."

"You have friends outside." After the doctor had gone, Lafayette kept saying the words to himself. They were the first comforting words he had heard for a long time.

His jailors had told him that nobody had tried to get him released from prison and that everyone had forgotten him. He was not sure now what the doctor had meant, or whether he trusted him. Yet he found himself looking forward impatiently to the doctor's next visit.

"The governor of the prison has graciously allowed me to bring you this book to read," the doctor said two days later. Then, when the guard seemed not to be watching, he whispered, "Hold page twenty-five to the fire."

The doctor smiled slightly as he felt Lafayette's pulse quicken under his fingers.

"I have told the governor of the prison that you will die unless you get out into the air," he said. "He has ordered that you shall be taken for a drive twice a week for a month. The drives will begin next week. In the meantime, take these pills before meals. And I'll look in on you tomorrow."

Lafayette could hardly wait until he was alone again. With shaking hands he held page twenty-five to his feeble charcoal fire. Secret writing slowly became visible. There was writing in the margins.

I met you when I was a very small child. I am Francis Huger of South Carolina, the son of your first host in America. With me is Dr. Bollman, unknown to you but your sincere admirer. We have made plans to rescue you. The doctor does not know all, but will smuggle notes.

There was no more room on the page. But

the message had been enough to make Lafayette feel almost dizzy. It had been so long since he had felt a spark of hope, or had even dreamed of escape.

As the doctor had prescribed, Lafayette was now driven out under close guard twice a week. Escape must be made on one of these drives. The day was agreed upon.

One November day, the carriage left the fortress. A soldier sat beside the driver. A guard sat on the seat with Lafayette.

How good the fresh air smelled to a man so long confined in a damp dungeon! Lafayette felt uncaged. His pulse quickened as he heard the approach of horsemen behind him. Two young men reined their horses to a walk as they passed the carriage. They saw Lafayette wipe his forehead with his handkerchief. This was a signal which had been agreed upon.

At some distance from the fortress, the horsemen turned and passed the carriage again. Lafayette knew that they would now follow it. The next move was his.

"The doctor says I have great need of ex-

This was the signal agreed upon

ercise," he told the guard. "Is it permitted that
I get out and walk about for a few minutes?"

The guard had been told that this could be
allowed. The carriage stopped, and he and Lafayette got out and paced back and forth.

Lafayette listened. He heard hoofbeats.

"That is a fine sword you are wearing," he
said, reaching for the hilt of the guard's sword.

The guard wrenched his sword away. He
was about to draw it, when Lafayette leaped on
him and tried to throw him to the ground.

"Help!" screamed the guard.

Lafayette's fist came up and caught him in
the mouth. The guard bit, and blood trickled
down Lafayette's clothes from his own hand.
The two horsemen leaped from their saddles.
One, who hardly looked more than a boy, ran
to help Lafayette overpower the guard. The
other chased the soldier who was running in
the direction of the prison. Frightened by the
confusion and shouting, one of the riderless
horses bolted.

"I'm Huger," gasped the young man who
was struggling with the guard. "I've got him

down. I can handle him. Take my horse and go to Hoff. Hurry. Go to Hoff."

Lafayette swung to the saddle and galloped away. He thought the young man had said, "Go off," not, "Go to Hoff." Lafayette knew a carriage was waiting somewhere to take him over the Austrian frontier. He did not know it was waiting at the town of Hoff.

Soon he came to a crossroads. He hesitated, then took the road to the right. He did not realize for some time that he must have taken the wrong road. The afternoon dimmed into darkness. He should have come to the waiting carriage long ago. He knew he was lost. He must find a fresh horse and a guide to the frontier.

"I'm a merchant and have lost my way to the border," he told a peasant. But when the suspicious peasant brought Austrian soldiers instead of a guide, he was recognized.

"The minute I saw his bloody coat I knew he was no merchant," the peasant boasted.

The next day Lafayette was taken back to prison.

CHAPTER FIFTEEN

Unexpected Visitors

POOR Lafayette! Now he was not even allowed to have a candle in his prison cell. Day after day he sat in dreary darkness. Even the guards refused to speak unless they had something unpleasant to tell him.

"What has become of the two young men who tried to help me?" he asked.

"Hanged, of course," said one of the guards.

Another day a jailor told him about the machine for cutting off heads that was being used in Paris.

"They call it a guillotine. They've cut off the King's head and the Queen's. Hundreds of heads. Thousands of heads. And a good thing, too. There'll be fewer Frenchmen for us Austrians to conquer."

Talk like that naturally did not raise Lafayette's spirits. The poor King and Queen, he thought. He knew they had been unwise, but he had never believed them to be wicked. Dreadful things must be taking place in France. He worried a great deal about his family.

One afternoon he heard keys turn in the locks. It was not time for a meal. Nobody ever visited his tomblike cell. Who could it be?

He heard light footsteps and the heavy tread of the guard. The cell door opened. He looked up. Sudden tears filled his eyes. He could not speak. There stood his wife, Adrienne, with his daughters, Anastasie and Virginie.

"Gilbert!"

"Father!"

"Thank God you're alive!" cried Lafayette, putting his arms around his wife. "Let me look at you. You haven't changed, my dear wife. But the girls have grown into young ladies."

There stood his wife and two daughters

"I wish we came bringing news of your release," said Adrienne. "I saw the Emperor of Austria and begged him to let you go. He won't set you free. But he will let us live with you in prison."

"But you and the girls can't stay in this wretched place," said Lafayette.

"We *are* staying," insisted Adrienne. "I shall never leave you again."

Suddenly Lafayette had a worried thought. "Where's George?" he asked, almost dreading to hear.

"Quite safe," replied his wife. "I sent him to America. He's with Washington. The Americans have been kind. Oh, but you're so thin, Gilbert! And your poor clothes! It's lucky I brought my embroidery silks with me, so I can mend the holes in your coat."

They had supper together after a while. Then the girls went to bed in the next cell and Lafayette and Adrienne were allowed to sit and talk for an hour. Adrienne told him then about the dreadful days of terror and bloodshed in France. Tears rolled down her cheeks when she told how her mother, aunt, and grandmother had been killed by the guillotine.

"The men in power seemed out of their minds," she told her husband. "They killed everybody they disliked or envied. Everybody who disagreed with them. After a time it seemed that they killed just for the sake of killing. Nobody was safe. Nobody."

"What did you do, my dear wife?"

"At first I was allowed to stay at Chavaniac. The villagers were very kind to me. But the Jacobins could not bear to let the wife of Lafayette live in comfort. So I was taken to Paris.

"They put me in prison, Gilbert, in the school you first went to in Paris. It was made into a prison. Afterwards, they put me into another prison where people every day were thrown into carts and taken to be guillotined." She shuddered. "I always expected to be next," she said.

Lafayette took her hand and held it tightly.

"It's better in France now," she went on. "The cruel leaders of the Jacobins finally met the same death they had brought upon so many others. The killing stopped then. And James Monroe, who is now the American minister to France, was able to get me released from prison."

"And here you are in prison again," Lafayette sighed.

"But we're together," said Adrienne.

Then Lafayette told her how near he had come, the year before, to escaping from prison. "Those two brave young men who tried to help me escape gave their lives for me," he said. "They were hanged."

"But they weren't!" cried Adrienne. "I know all about it, for I received a letter from Francis Huger after he got back to America. They were kept in prison six months and then released."

"Then the guards lied!" said Lafayette. "I'm so happy that the two young men are still alive."

Now that his family were with him, prison life seemed less hard to Lafayette. Adrienne had money to buy him better food. Yet there were still shreds of tobacco in the stew and hairs in the soup. Nor were the Lafayettes allowed to have forks to eat with. It was harsh living for them all.

After breakfast every morning, the family were locked into Lafayette's cell. He was allowed to have a few books now. He often read aloud while the girls and their mother sewed.

"Stop a minute, please, Father," Anastasie said one day. "I want to measure your foot." She was making him a pair of slippers out of the stout cloth of her mother's corset. For his boots had great holes in both soles.

Two years went by. Time went fast now that he was not alone, Lafayette told his family. In spite of discomforts, they laughed and joked. Anastasie even drew comic pictures of one of their jailors.

One morning, after Lafayette had been a prisoner for five years, the governor of the prison sent for him. The governor was much more polite than usual. "I suppose you know France has defeated Austria," he said.

"I knew from what I've overheard from the

guards that our countries were not still at war," said Lafayette.

"France wouldn't have beaten Austria if it hadn't been for that young French general, Napoleon Bonaparte," muttered the governor. "I don't know why, but it seems that General Bonaparte made it one of the conditions of the peace treaty that you should be set free. In short, Marquis de Lafayette, you and your family may leave here tomorrow afternoon at two o'clock."

The next afternoon a pale, thin man with a happy face helped his wife and two daughters into a carriage in the prison courtyard. He told the coachman to drive them to the Austrian frontier. From there they would take another coach and go to Danish territory where they could stay with friends. For, although he was out of prison, Lafayette was not yet allowed to return to France.

"But I'm free," he said joyfully, as the coach rolled along. "How lovely free air is to breathe! How bright the sun is! What a lovely world it is outside prison!"

CHAPTER SIXTEEN

Lafayette and Napoleon

Do YOU and George have to go to Paris
again tomorrow?" asked Lafayette's daughter,
Virginie.

"I'm afraid so," replied Lafayette.

It was a lovely June evening many years
later. The Lafayette family were at dinner.
George and his wife, and Anastasie and Virginie and their husbands were all living with
Lafayette at La Grange. This country estate
was forty-five miles from Paris. It had been Lafayette's home since he had been allowed to
return to France.

Today, he looked about the table with
pride, thinking how happy he was to have his
family with him. Yet, as always, he missed

Adrienne, who had died several years ago. Lafayette sighed, as he remembered that Adrienne had never fully recovered from the hardships she had suffered while she stayed with him in prison.

"Since George and Father have been elected to the National Assembly, they're in Paris almost as much as they are here," said George's wife.

"The National Assembly is now called the Chamber of Deputies, my dear," George reminded her. "Now that Napoleon allows representatives of the people to help govern the country, we deputies have a great responsibility."

Virginie saw that her father was not eating much of his dinner. "Don't you find the beefsteak tender?" she asked.

"It's delicious," replied Lafayette. But he soon laid down his fork. He was too worried to be hungry.

Lafayette had been able to do very little for the people of France since he had come to La Grange. For Napoleon Bonaparte had made himself Emperor of the country. And Napoleon was a dictator who had ruled with no help from the people.

Unfortunately, the Emperor Napoleon had not been content to rule France alone. He had tried to conquer half the world. He had led the armies of France into war after war.

At first he had won nearly every battle which he and his armies had fought. Then he had begun to lose battles. Since he was afraid that this would turn the people of France against him, he had allowed them to hold free elections once more. Recently he had given the Chamber of Deputies power to make laws.

Now England, Austria, and Germany had all united against Napoleon. They were preparing to invade France. And he was on his way to Belgium with an army to meet them in battle. Lafayette was deeply worried about the outcome of this battle.

"The English have grown strong while we have grown weak," Lafayette told his family, later that evening. "I wish I could feel more hopeful about our chance of victory. But one thing I am sure of. This must be the last time Napoleon is allowed to lead French troops into battle. The country is sick of war, half ruined by war. We need years of peace if France is to become a strong nation again."

The next morning, Lafayette and George drove by coach to Paris. There they found people excited about the battle Napoleon intended to fight at Waterloo in Belgium. Many people thought that it might be going on already. Anxiously, all Paris waited for news from the battlefield.

Lafayette and George were at breakfast several days later, when a friend came hastily into the room.

"Napoleon has *lost* the battle of Waterloo!" he cried. "The victorious armies are marching toward Paris. And the Chamber of Deputies is meeting at once to decide what must be done."

Lafayette and George hurried to the Chamber of Deputies. In the hall where the deputies met, men stood about, talking excitedly.

"Napoleon rode ahead of the victorious armies and is now in Paris," said one of the deputies to Lafayette. "He is demanding that he be made dictator again."

Lafayette's face was grave. "I never trusted Napoleon," he said. "Now we know that he was only pretending to let the representatives of the people govern France. So he demands to be dictator again! He intends to rule again without the help of the Chamber of Deputies. Not if I have anything to say about it!"

When the Chamber of Deputies was called to order, Napoleon's brother Lucien stood up and made a fiery speech. Napoleon could still save France, he said, if he were given more troops, more power.

"Your Emperor needs your confidence, your trust. He alone can save France," Lucien pleaded.

Some of the deputies seemed persuaded that they should give Napoleon all he asked. Then Lafayette rose to his feet.

"France," said Lafayette calmly, "has left the bones of her soldiers in the sands of Egypt, in Spain, in Italy, Austria, on the cold Russian plains. The nation has followed the Emperor on fifty fields of battle. Two million men have fallen for the sake of one man who wished to fight all Europe. It is enough!"

"Bravo," shouted hundreds of voices. And there was no more talk about raising another army for Napoleon.

It was several months before Lafayette and George made ready to return to La Grange. They had lived through sad days in Paris. Lafayette and other members of the Chamber of Deputies had forced Napoleon to give up his throne and leave the country. And they had watched the victorious armies march into Paris. Then the countries which had defeated France had put King Louis XVIII on the throne.

One September morning, Lafayette climbed wearily into the coach which was to take him back to La Grange. He felt very much discouraged. Lafayette knew and disliked this fat king, Louis XVIII. Under him, Lafayette felt sure that there would be little freedom in France.

They had forced Napoleon to give up

"Sometimes, George," said Lafayette, "I give up hope that France will ever be a free country."

"That doesn't sound like you, Father," said George. "You must be tired."

When father and son reached La Grange, nobody met them at the door. From an upstairs room they heard a baby crying. George ran up the stairs two steps at a time. Lafayette followed more slowly. And there in a pleasant room, he saw George bending over his new baby boy.

"His name is Oscar Thomas Gilbert Motier de Lafayette," said George proudly. "But you may call him Gilbert, if you like, Father. I wish he were being born into a freer France, poor little one."

"France *will* be free some day," said Lafayette, suddenly full of hope again. "I believe that with all my heart. By the time this child grows to manhood, France will have as free a government as my beloved adopted country, the United States of America."

CHAPTER SEVENTEEN

"*Welcome, Lafayette!*"

ON A bright spring day in the year 1824, Lafayette sat in his study reading a letter. He glanced up as Virginie entered the room.

"You're looking very happy today, Father," she said.

"Spring at La Grange always makes for happiness," said Lafayette. "Nowhere is spring more beautiful. I am also pleased today by a letter I have just received from America. The President of the United States has sent me a most cordial invitation to visit America."

"And will you go?" Virginie asked. "Really, Father, I think you should."

"It will be no duty but a great pleasure," said Lafayette. "I never dreamed when I left

America that over forty years would pass before I should return."

He sat back in his chair thinking of the young Lafayette in the young nation, the United States of America. "There's no doubt that the years have greatly changed us both." He chuckled. "I'm afraid, my dear, that age does not improve a man as much as it does a nation."

"Nonsense, Father! You're in as good health and spirits as you ever were," declared Virginie.

"Thank you, my dear," said Lafayette. "If I seem young for my years it's because I'm surrounded by the love of my family."

Virginie smiled. The family would miss him, she thought, if he went on a long visit to America. Yet while he was there they would not have to worry about his getting into trouble with King Louis XVIII.

The King was so afraid that Lafayette might force him to give up his throne that he paid men to write and print wicked lies about him. Yet even the King could not stop people

In New York he was met with cheers

from loving Lafayette. For they knew Lafayette to be a lover of liberty.

At last the day came for Lafayette to leave for America. He had decided to take George with him. Affectionately, he said good-by to his children and grandchildren at La Grange. Then he and George rode to the port from which they were to sail.

Hundreds of men, women, and children were there to see him off. The King's troops pushed them back from the dock. Yet, as a rowboat took Lafayette out to the frigate, cries of *"Vive Lafayette!"* rang out. To the French people Lafayette was still a great hero.

Lafayette soon found that he was well remembered in America. At the end of the voyage across the Atlantic, he landed in New York. There he was met with roaring cannon, waving flags, playing bands, and people cheering themselves hoarse. As he got into a coach drawn by four white horses, that was to take him to City Hall, he heard the driver say to one of the horses, "Behave pretty now, Charlie. You're going to carry the greatest man in the world."

Lafayette smiled.

"Of course I'm far from being that," he told George with a chuckle. "But how pleasant it is to hear someone say such a thing!"

Cheering crowds lined the streets through which Lafayette's carriage passed. Nearly everybody wore a white or blue ribbon badge with Lafayette's picture on it. Signs and banners in every shopwindow carried the words, "Welcome, Lafayette!" And Lafayette heard these same words shouted over and over.

New York's warm welcome was repeated in city after city, town after town. In Boston he passed under an archway put up in his honor.

Even small towns and villages celebrated when he passed through them. One day, as his carriage halted at a village green, two small boys came close to him.

"See my badge, Mister Lafayette?" asked the taller boy. "Johnny don't have no badge, but I've got one." And he pointed to the white ribbon he was wearing with Lafayette's picture printed on it.

The smaller boy dug his bare feet in the dusty road. He did not look up. His underlip was quivering. Lafayette reached out and took off the little boy's cap. The youngster's curly red hair shone in the sun.

"His red hair is all the badge he needs," said Lafayette. "My hair used to be as red as yours, my boy."

The country had grown since Lafayette had left it many years earlier. Then there had been only thirteen states. Now there were twenty-four. He traveled by coach and by steamboat. He saw much of America and found it a fair and prosperous land.

"Aren't you exhausted, Father?" George asked him one day.

"I am enjoying myself so much, I haven't time to be tired," said Lafayette.

He enjoyed visiting his friends, Jefferson and Madison, in Virginia. And he stood again at Yorktown, remembering the battles with the British there. "It makes me happy to realize that I had a small part in building this great nation," he told George.

The time came when he stood at the tomb of his beloved George Washington. He remembered how kind Washington had always been. He remembered how bravely Washington had fought for his country.

"I have always tried to act as I thought he would in my place," Lafayette said to himself. And he left the tomb with tears in his eyes.

Lafayette spent a year in America. Children were named after him, and hotels, colleges, towns, boats, hospitals, city squares. He would live in name in every state in the Union.

America gave him gifts. Two hundred thousand dollars were voted him by Congress to repay him for the money he had so generously given when the country had needed it most. And from grateful citizens he received umbrellas, canes, waistcoats, a coat, waterproof boots. There was even a wampum necklace from his friends, the Iroquois Indians. And somebody brought him something truly American—a grizzly bear!

Lafayette's sixty-eighth birthday was celebrated at the White House. President Adams made a speech in his honor. When he had finished speaking, Lafayette replied.

"God bless you, sir, and all who surround you," he said. "God bless the American people, each of their states, and the Federal Government. Accept this patriotic farewell of an overflowing heart."

He sailed for France the next day in the American frigate, *Brandywine,* named for the first battle he fought in America.

After having seen America, Lafayette was going back to France more determined than ever to renew his fight for a democratic government. "I must persuade the young men of France to fight for liberty," he thought. "France, too, must soon take her place among the free nations of the world."

The American sailors on the *Brandywine* often discussed their famous passenger.

"He's a great man, all right," said one sailor.

"That's so," said another. "He's a great man in the United States and a great man in France, too. I guess a man has to be *really* great to be a hero in two countries."

SIGNATURE BOOKS are the true life-stories of real boys and girls who grew up to be famous men and women. These books tell of the many exciting adventures of those boys and girls when they were growing up, and what they did to make themselves remembered.

Leading authors and artists have worked together to give you the thrilling stories of these interesting people. If you liked the story you have just read, you will enjoy reading the books listed below and on the next page.

SIGNATURE BOOKS

"Names that Made History"

ENID LAMONTE MEADOWCROFT, *Supervising Editor*

THE STORY OF BUFFALO BILL
By Edmund Collier.   *Illustrated by Nicholas Eggenhofer*

THE STORY OF CHRISTOPHER COLUMBUS
By Nina Brown Baker.   *Illustrated by David Hendrickson*

THE STORY OF DAVY CROCKETT
By Enid LaMonte Meadowcroft.   *Illustrated by C. B. Falls*

THE STORY OF THOMAS ALVA EDISON
By Enid LaMonte Meadowcroft.   *Illustrated by Harve Stein*